The Faith we See

The Faith we See

Working with Images of Christ

Janet Hodgson

Copyright © Janet Hodgson 2006
Cover photography © Robert Cooper

British Library Cataloguing in Publication data

A catalogue record for this book is available
from the British Library

ISBN 1-85852-309-5 and 978-1-85852-309-5

First published by Inspire
4 John Wesley Road
Werrington
Peterborough PE4 6ZP

Printed and bound in Great Britain by
Aldridge Print Group, Mitcham, Surrey

Preface

This book is about working with pictures or images of Christ as a way of enabling people to explore, nurture and share their faith in order to further the mission of God (*missio Dei*). Over the years I have read innumerable books about mission, written from every imaginable perspective. Almost without exception they have been written by clergy for clergy. The assumption seems to be that however you define mission, it is the clergy who will have the vision, the clergy who will take the leadership roles, and the clergy who will have the expertise in the strategic planning and actual work of mission.

As a lay person myself, I have written this book for both clergy and lay people. My hope is that no matter who you are you will be enthused to work with images of Christ as an imaginative and original way of becoming involved in the mission of God, enthusiasm being understood as the divine indwelling (*en theo*) of the Holy Spirit. At the same time, clergy might well have an additional role in enabling lay people to have the space and the freedom to do this work, and in giving them the necessary encouragement and assistance along the way.

The laity has much to offer the Church in terms of their gifts and experience, all of which are precious in the sight of God. I believe that all people, both clergy and lay, have a calling from God to carry out his mission and his ministry in the world around us. Each one of us has a unique vocation and, while these are all varied, all are of value.

Many people already have the *The Christ We Share* resource pack or CD-ROM, containing images of Christ from around the world, together with the *Born Among Us* pack, exploring images of the nativity of Christ in a global context. This material was published by the Methodist Church together with the Anglican Church Mission Society and the United Society for the Propagation of the Gospel (USPG) in Britain and Ireland, and is an invaluable basic resource. I hope to complement the emphasis on world mission in these packs by showing how an expanded collection of images might be used for personal faith development, spiritual enrichment, evangelism and mission, meditation and worship, and the living out of the gospel in a local context.

The more recent CD-ROM, *Images of Salvation: the story of the Bible through medieval art*, from St John's College, Nottingham, depicts past images of Christ in different biblical settings. Some people may already have their own collections of images, or be blessed with a church which is rich in such imagery, or might even be inspired to start making their own collection. Whether you already have some material or none, this book is designed to encourage you to find new ways of exploring and sharing your faith through working with the images and so follow in the way of our Lord and Saviour Jesus Christ.

My own work in mission is based on a lifetime's experience, in South Africa and in Britain. For 12 years I lectured part-time in the Department of Religious Studies in the University of Cape Town in the sociology of religion, gospel and culture, African Traditional Religions and Christianity, and the history of mission. At the same time, I organized adult education courses in my Anglican country parish. This led to diocesan involvement in mission, and for 10 years I was the only woman and lay person on the Provincial Board of Mission of the (Anglican) Church of the Province of Southern Africa. My postgraduate studies were based on fieldwork which took me to every corner of the country but focused especially on the Xhosa-speaking area from which Nelson Mandela hails. This gave me a privileged insight into the lives, beliefs, socio-political history and experiences of an extraordinary range of people during a time of upheaval, suffering and struggle spanning the last half of the apartheid years.

After moving to England at the end of 1987, I was for a year and a half the first Visiting Fellow at the College of the Ascension in Selly Oak, Birmingham. The College (united later with the Methodist Church) was run by the USPG, an Anglican mission society that celebrated its tercentenary in 2001. This was an invaluable opportunity to meet people from all over the world and my fascination with seeing how Christ has been incarnated in different cultures and contexts dates from this time. I went on to serve the USPG for five years, first as Area Secretary in the Oxford Diocese, and then as Field Worker in the Dioceses of Oxford and St Albans. Although my brief was overseas mission, such were the misconceptions about mission in general that this had to be the starting point for my work.

The last seven years of my British experience was as Adviser in Local Mission for the Diocese of Durham. This was a hugely creative and happy time in which I was able to develop and implement a number of different models of mission, which I had been exploring for many years. A fruitful partnership with Revd Canon Robert Warren, initially National Adviser for the board of Mission of the Church of England, and subsequently a member of the Springboard team, the Archbishops' Initiative in Evangelism, led to some of my thinking about mission being used nationally. A bonus was the fun we had working together. I am indebted to him for the Foreword to this book.

Since my time at Selly Oak in the 1980s I have continued to expand the way I work with images of Christ. I have now built up a collection of more than 4,000 pictures encompassing both historic images from down the centuries and contemporary ones from around the world. I have used this resource with all the mainline denominations across England and Wales and in every imaginable context – urban, rural, inner-city, suburban, inter-faith, multicultural, clerical and lay (separately and together), parish, deanery and diocesan, as well as with groups of women, children and youth, prayer and Bible study groups, meditation groups, baptism preparation, lay training, theological institutions, Lent and Advent courses, workshops, large and small conferences – and with a cross-section of people in Canada and South Africa, including indigenous people.

This book has been written as a response to all those people who have asked me to put my experience down on paper so that it could be shared more widely. The stories I have used have been drawn from a range of situations, but most names have been changed.

I would like to give a special word of thanks to all those who have encouraged me in this work over the years, especially Geoff Lowson, formerly Mission Adviser for USPG in the north-east of England and now Priest in Charge of Tynemouth Priory, Stephen Conway, Archdeacon of Durham, Michael Turnbull, former Bishop of Durham, and Alan Smithson, former Bishop of Jarrow. Bishop Alan and Robert Cooper both contributed to the writing of the manuscript.

Mention must also be made of a number of clergy across the full spectrum of Anglican traditions and other denominations who were unstinting in their support, especially the diocesan missioners and evangelists in our close-knit fellowship in the north of England. Another source of great encouragement was the team of lay Mission Enablers with whom I worked in Durham Diocese, who have remained friends. Most of them have built up their own collections of images and have continued to use them to good effect. But above all, Bishop Michael had the grace and trust to give me the freedom to spread my wings as missioner, for which I am eternally grateful, while Brenda Turnbull gave sterling practical assistance.

In South Africa, I must thank Billy Kennedy, Director of Temenos Retreat Centre in McGregor, for his contribution, and my friends and family, who all played a vital part in giving me the necessary support and encouragement in the writing of the book.

Putting together the CD-ROM was a major undertaking which could not have been achieved without the help of friends. My thanks to Robert Cooper and Paul Judson in Durham, and Geoff Neill and Marianne Saddington in McGregor, for all their hard work. Above all, I am indebted to Dr Natalie Watson, Head of Publishing at Inspire, who not only helped with tracking down images for the CD-ROM but who put me on course for the writing of this book and kept her faith in me along the way. I would also like to thank Susan Hibbins at Inspire for her work on the text.

Finally, I am grateful for the friendship, wisdom and support of Jayant Kothare, whose ministry as an Anglican parish priest in Handsworth, Southall, Thamesmead and New Moston in north Manchester added much to my knowledge of multiracial, multicultural, multifaith Britain. Our many open conversations over 18 years have been most stimulating, and his wide experience of the World Church and his extensive reading have fed into my writing some seminal insights into theology, mission and worship. I am also indebted to him for his helpful critique and input in editing early drafts of this manuscript.

Janet Hodgson
May 2006

Foreword

The Christian faith is like a precious jewel. It has many faces. As cultures turn, change, decay or develop, different faces of the jewel of the gospel shine light on that changing context. This means that the Church is called to be continually listening to both the *context* and the (gospel) *content* to discern how the one speaks to the other.

This can be seen in today's world. We are living in a culture where *visual* communication (associated with all that is meant by 'the media') has become more dominant than the solely *verbal*. The number of videos available in Public Libraries is evidence of this. Another way in which contemporary culture is changing is evident in a shift from a rational, logic, analytical and verbal form – associated with the right hemisphere of the brain – to a more intuitive, imaginative, holistic and visual form – associated with the left hemisphere of the brain.

All of this represents a call to the Church to think creatively about how faith is communicated. It is this that makes this book such an important contribution to the faith and life of Christians and the Christian Church; for it is all about a visual and an imaginative/intuitive way of exploring and expressing faith. Not that this is a new 'theoretical model'; rather it is a story of one person's lifelong exploration of working with images of Christ as a way to provoke ideas about faith and to provoke people to articulate those ideas.

Janet brings to this story a vast collection of images of Christ from across the globe and down the centuries of the Christian tradition, as well as a rich experience of using this approach with people in both the Northern and Southern hemispheres. I have been privileged to be present when Janet has worked in this way, and I can testify to the fact that it has felt like being in a master-class. Janet has a deep empathy with people, a wonderful skill in provoking fresh ways of looking at images and at the faith they seek to express, a determined commitment to enable people (particularly lay people) to give expression to their faith, and a lively passion for the task. No description of Janet's skills would be complete without an acknowledgement of the enthusiasm and passion she has for working with people; and her desire that people should have fun while exploring faith in this way.

All these skills are now made available to the reader so that this book will undoubtedly help to raise up a new generation of people able to work in this creative, visual and passionate way. I commend it warmly as both a lively description of one person's way of working with images of Christ and as a practical down-to-earth 'how to' guide. I have no doubt that this book, born out of a lifetime's experience, will bear rich fruit in the articulation, development and passing on of the faith in God as it is revealed in Christ.

Revd Canon Robert Warren

Contents

1

Why Images of Christ?

Telling the story

John was dying of cancer. He knew he had not long to live but found it hard to talk about his illness let alone share his feelings or his faith. His was a small village community in north-east England, with a supportive, tightly knit circle of friends. But John was imprisoned by his English reserve. Neither his priest nor his family could penetrate his defences. Then he attended a Lenten series of evenings in which we worked with images of Christ and, miraculously, he was released from his emotional captivity. In fact, once he began talking there was no stopping him. But first a word of explanation as to what the images are about.

As on this occasion, an introductory session with any new group of people is based on a display of pictures or symbolic representations of Christ from over the centuries and around the world. The images vary in size from postcard to A4, and include copies of paintings in every possible medium – pastel, watercolour, oils, charcoal, chalk, acrylic, aquatint, gouache, tempera, pen and wash. There are also pictures of sculptures in metal, marble, stone, wire, cement, and sand; and of wood carvings, bronzes, ceramics, calligraphy, manuscript illuminations, linocuts, woodcuts, etchings, ivories, icons, collages, banners, batiks, embroideries, tapestries, stained-glass windows, frescoes, murals, mosaics, crosses and crucifixes, posters, prayer cards, internet images, abstracts, symbolic designs, word pictures and biblical texts. There are more than 4,000 images in my collection but I usually draw from a core selection of a couple of hundred pictures which offer a comprehensive range of material.

Some portrayals of Christ are hundreds of years old and span successive ages of religious art across Europe, with ancient Coptic images from Ethiopia providing a more exotic element. The majority, however, are modern and encompass a global Christology, contemporary western imagery being as challenging as that from Asia, Africa and Latin America. A good number of the images concentrate on the figure of Christ, more especially his face. Others depict snapshots or scenes from his life, teaching and ministry. They have been conceived in every imaginable context and every possible cultural setting, ranging from the lifelike to the abstract.

Together the images represent the incarnate God in a rich diversity of moods and modes, challenging us to see Christ afresh, whether we are churchgoers or not. For those accustomed to wrestling with questions of faith at a cerebral level, the visual impact of the images opens up a surprising new world of experience which can reach into the very depths of their being. This is all about 'seeing with the eyes of the heart': a spiritual exploration that engages one's most intimate feelings and brings one closer to God. At the same time, the images encompass both the particularity and the universality of the life of Christ, offering amazing new insights into 'the greatest story ever told'.

However, a church hall is not the most inviting setting for doing this sort of work. Strictly functional in its furnishing and bereft of any decoration bar the latest Sunday school offerings, it is an uphill struggle to create a welcoming ambience. Add to this the cold, wet, windy northern weather and it says much for the commitment of the faithful that so many turned up for the first night of the Lenten course. When it came to selecting an image, John chose a picture of the peaceful young face of a crucified African Christ from the Cameroons, crowned with thorns. This was the trigger that unlocked him from his spiritual straitjacket.

Gathered together in small groups, the participants took turns in talking about who Christ was for them in their chosen pictures. For John, it was the youthfulness of the African Christ that had pierced his heart. In contrast, he felt that he had had a good, long life and was now ready to die. For him, too, the serenity which this image portrayed had given him the assurance of an eternal peace beyond understanding. With tears streaming down his face, John was at last able to share his innermost feelings about his illness and his approaching death.

This was not the end of the story. As Holy Week approached, John was invited to join those who were to have their feet washed at the Maundy Thursday service, a first in the village church. Initially John would have none of it, but, after working with images of Christ washing his disciples' feet, he changed his mind. On Maundy Thursday he came forward with the other eleven parishioners and duly had his feet washed. This was the last time he attended church. He died on Easter Monday. At his funeral, his priest told the story of how the image of a crucified African Christ had liberated John in his final weeks, holding the picture up in the pulpit for all to see.

John's story shows how powerful working with images of Christ can be. There is the initial impact, when an image seems to speak directly to you, unlocking your feelings and helping you to articulate your faith. But it doesn't stop there. Many people retain the image in their memories, and they experience an ongoing dialogue with the image in the weeks ahead as it continues its work of transformation from within. All speak of being changed by the experience, and of their joy in coming to a new understanding of their faith, however tentative and unstructured that may be.

For John, the picture of an African Christ helped him find peace during his last days, and it also inspired him to keep growing in faith right up to the end, enabling him to face new challenges with extraordinary good humour. His story has been told countless times; it greatly affected his family and friends, and it also touched an ever-widening circle of strangers, like the ripples that emanate outwards when you drop a pebble in a pond.

John's story is special but not unique. Recently I met a woman who had worked with the images during a parish retreat some seven years previously. She had chosen a contemporary picture of a crucified Christ with a crowd of onlookers at the foot of the cross. This image has remained imprinted on her memory to this day, as fresh as when she first saw it, inspiring in her the faith to cope with her exacting job as a senior administrator in social work.

Another older woman had been deeply affected by a painting by Edward Burne-Jones (1833-98) called *The Merciful Knight*. Here, the Christ figure, naked except for a loin cloth and with his feet impaled, leans forward from the cross to embrace the kneeling figure of a knight. The knight, clothed in shining black armour, has laid down sword and helmet to receive the kiss of Christ. Although the picture might speak of Victorian sentimentality, for this woman the image of Christ's healing touch to one who is defenceless and seeks forgiveness, released her from the burdens of a tortured past. She has now taken up a whole new area of work with abused women and children. Images which portray Christ with the woman taken in adultery have had a similar liberating effect on both men and women, often reducing them to tears as they experience the grace of God in offering them a new life.

One of the most powerful images in my collection is the barbed wire crucifix from South Africa. It was originally fashioned in a workshop during the darkest days of apartheid, when the rolls of barbed wire which encircled every African township symbolized the siege mentality of the Afrikaner government. These Boer descendants had seemingly forgotten the enduring legacy of bitterness and hatred left by their erstwhile British enemies. Barbed wire had been used during the Boer War to contain women and children in concentration camps, where hundreds died of disease and hunger. Seventy years later, the barbed wire crucifix allowed this symbol of oppression to be transformed by Christ's suffering on the cross and become a subversive image which instilled hope and courage in all who saw it. Moreover, this image has taken on a universal meaning which speaks powerfully to people who have no knowledge of its past connotations. In Britain it has been incorporated in the Durham Diocesan AIDS logo.

An equally strong image from Africa is the simple cross which John Majok, a pastor living in a refugee camp in Sudan, moulded into the mud wall at the foot of his bed and on which he focused his daily prayers. Christian Aid has used it, together with a prayer for justice by Janet Morley, to publicize the plight of the Sudanese people. Again, this image has touched many lives, and people have been overwhelmed by the simplicity and steadfastness of John Majok's faith in the face of never-ending persecution and deprivation.

But the images are not only about pain and suffering. Many invite joy and celebration, comfort and trust, or an outpouring of love and devotion. What they have in common, though, is the way I work with them. I have designed a wide variety of exercises using images of Christ to enable people of all ages and of diverse backgrounds, situations, cultures and contexts to discover Christ for themselves and experience him in their lives; to get in touch with their innate spirituality and allow it to connect with their deepest feelings; to feel free to express their faith in ordinary everyday language and be confident in sharing it; and to be enthusiastic about living it.

In the exercises people are invited to explore their own understanding of Christ, often for the first time in their lives. In sharing their discoveries they offer each other an empathetic ear, non-judgemental encouragement and loving support as they experience the freedom of discerning challenging new dimensions of their faith and spirituality.

The basic exercise: 'Who do you say I am?'

Working with images of Christ is all about liberating people to take respons-ibility for their own spiritual journey. I start with a foundational exercise in which

an extensive range of pictures, from across the ages and around the globe, is displayed. The bigger the group the more pictures that are needed, and it is best to have the display tables well spaced around the venue so that people can spread out and have easy access to the images. The use of standing exhibition panels is effective as long as the pictures can be peeled off, but with a crowd the panels are impractical on their own.

In churches it is possible to spread pictures along pews, but the restricted access needs careful management. The vagaries of the congregation may also pose difficulties: during a service I have had parishioners sit on top of the pictures because they were on their customary seats! Moveable chairs work better than pews as they can be arranged in different formations according to available space. But any accessible surface area can be used, including low window sills, chests, the tops of display cabinets, side tables, and kneelers placed end to end along the altar rail. Care must always be taken to ensure that the pictures are well lit and arranged so that they are all clearly visible.

Ideally, participants sit in a circle to facilitate group sharing. A big group can be divided into a number of smaller groups of six to eight people, 10 at most. There is value in keeping a larger group such as a PCC together; but extra time must be allotted so that everyone can have their say. Comfortable seating helps people to relax so sitting in pews should be avoided if at all possible. If it cannot, small groups of four to six people can be seated together in adjacent pews with sharing taking place across them rather than laterally along long lines.

Warmth is important in cold weather and coolness in the heat. Heating in churches is often insufficient and needs to be taken into account when planning a workshop. On a cold winter's day, I vividly remember 600 people shivering miserably in Coventry Cathedral as they tried to cope with a malfunctioning heating system. In hot weather pictures mounted on card can start to curl. Rough handling of the images can also be a problem.

Timing for each part of the exercise is flexible and depends on the overall length of the workshop and the number of people involved. People should not feel rushed at any stage of the experience. In working out a timetable, allow spare time to deal with any unexpected needs which may require an immediate response. You might also want to mention how much time will be allowed for each section of the programme before it begins.

The workshop begins with introductions. The leader introduces himself or herself and then goes round the circle inviting participants to say something about themselves. In a small group they might also like to say why they are there, e.g. 'my priest bulldozed me into coming'; 'this is our parish away-day'; 'it sounded interesting'; or even, 'I'm waiting to discover why.' This gives people some sort of benchmark against which to evaluate the experience at the end.

The formal proceedings start with the reading of a passage from Scripture –

Peter's confession of Christ: 'Who do you say I am?' (Matthew 16.13-16; Mark 8.27-29; Luke 9.18-20) A short theological reflection can be given by the leader if desired, followed by an explanation of what the images represent, with basic information about their historical, geographical, social, political and artistic content. The amount of information provided is determined by the purpose of the workshop. This is followed by a simple explanation of how the images are to be used: as a way of doing theology together, exploring one's personal spirituality, meditating, sharing one's faith, or whatever other intentions have been agreed upon. We return to a discussion of these different issues in subsequent chapters. stressful

I regularly use a dialogue devised by John Bell of the Iona community to relax people and insert a fun element into the proceedings. Entitled 'Our Image of Jesus', it has two characters, one blustering and pompous and the other more down to earth and a little snide, providing contrasting views of how we should 'get our image of Jesus right'.[1] The substance of the dialogue is meaty but the way it is presented always raises laughs. It helps the participants to feel that they have some sort of ownership of the workshop if they take the parts, while a parish group enjoys seeing their incumbent as one of the actors.

After the introduction, participants are invited to walk round the displays and have a good look at all the pictures. In itself this is an important part of the learning process and should be done slowly and quietly. Whatever people's cultural backgrounds are, the diversity of pictures can come as quite a shock, especially if they are accustomed to thinking of Jesus as blond, blue-eyed and fair-skinned. Some images of a suffering Christ may also be disturbing, and this can be mentioned before people look at the displays, so that they are prepared. Participants are free to pick the pictures up to see them more closely or read any relevant information that may be on the reverse side. However, it is often better to let the images speak for themselves without taking on board the artist's intention, to give free rein to the viewer's imagination, intuition and interpretation.

It must be emphasized that in no way are any of the images intended to be actual likenesses of Christ. A common mistake is to search for a picture of how someone thinks Christ looked. But each picture mirrors the artist's subjective imaging of some aspect of Jesus' persona, life, teaching or ministry, and may well be abstract or symbolic.

The participants are asked to select one or two images in response to the question:

Who is Christ for you at this very moment?

This can be difficult because of the huge choice. People often find it easier and more enjoyable doing the exercise a second time around. Choosing two images allows for either complementary or contrasting depictions of Christ. More than two becomes unwieldy and involves too much time in the sharing of reflections. This limitation needs to be strictly observed. People need to have an open mind and allow the images to speak to them before making their choice. Frequently, people are amazed at the choices they make: they open up entirely new avenues of thought and feeling, and the impact can be quite overwhelming.

There needs to be an awareness that some people find it difficult to work with imagery per se, maybe for theological or personal reasons. Others may have problems with anthropomorphic pictures of Christ or genuinely struggle to find an image with which they can resonate. This is where written words, texts, abstracts, or symbolic representations, such as a lighted candle, a Bible, bread and wine, a picture of a cross or people at worship, can help. The leader should be available to answer any questions. The only time I have been completely floored is when a young woman asked for a picture of a toothbrush to symbolize the cleansing properties of Christ.

People are asked to pick up their chosen pictures and return with them to their seats. Time is then given for silent meditation. Reflection on the pictures and an ensuing discussion is focused on two questions:

Why did you choose this particular image or images?

This may be because the image is artistically pleasing or historically interesting; or it is familiar and has sentimental associations; or because it resonates with a past or present experience, offers challenging new insights, or provides an opportunity to learn about another culture and identify with different experiences.

Who is Christ for you as reflected in your chosen pictures?

This question is far more difficult as it involves issues of faith and spirituality. However, it must be addressed or the whole point of the exercise is lost. Help and encouragement may be needed.

Sharing is initially done in pairs, encouraging trust and openness. A threesome may be formed if there are uneven numbers in a group and they will probably require more time. People should feel free to say what they want and not be under any pressure to go beyond what feels comfortable. It must be emphasized that the process is open-ended and that there are no right or wrong answers to the questions. Clergy may need to be gently reminded that they have no special status: some find it difficult to abdicate control but they can learn much by listening.

The leader checks that everyone understands what is required of them, and encourages those who are nervous or withdrawn. Care must be taken not to intrude upon private conversations; but it is helpful to see what images have been chosen and to make sure that all have an equal chance to share. At no time should the leader comment on discussions or provide any input unless invited. People can reach surprisingly deep levels of intimacy within a matter of minutes, even with complete strangers. The time allocated to the paired sharing will depend on the overall schedule, but 10-15 minutes is about average.

Everyone then joins together in one big circle or a few smaller ones depending on numbers, and the participants take turns to give personal reflections on the two discussion questions. The leader may need to encourage the less confident and to gently restrain the overly voluble. Again, people are free to share at whatever level feels comfortable to them and their input is usually briefer than in the paired conversations. If invited, a partner can assist in recalling important insights.

The larger the group the longer it will take for every person to have their say. After everyone has contributed, they place their images on the floor in front of them, building up a collective picture of who Christ is for the group as a whole. This is a learning experience, and time can be given to reflect on this corporate collection of images, to identify any themes that might have emerged, such as suffering, reconciliation or celebration, and to discuss the implications of this.

People then have a chance to reflect on their experience, to offer any comments about the pictures, to ask any questions, and to evaluate what they have learnt from the exercise. Participants should be warned that confidentiality about what has been shared during the exercise should be maintained afterwards. Making fun of someone's contribution or personal comments such as 'I cannot imagine why you chose that picture', or 'That was lousy theology' must be strenuously avoided.

Group leaders should be reminded that working with images is about affirming and empowering people in exploring their faith, and of the fragility of what may well be a radically new religious experience. Some clergy cannot resist offering a homily at the end of a workshop, nervous that the formularies of the Church might have been transgressed. This suggests an authoritarian leadership model and puts paid to any further open discussions. Where possible clergy should be discouraged from making comments about the process during the workshop. However, there is real value in their getting together afterwards with members of their faith community to evaluate the exercise. It is also useful if participants report back to their congregation either in a magazine article or during a service.

A word of warning. Some people think that the images can be taken away, or they become emotionally involved and cannot bear to part with them. The fact that they are part of a personal collection needs to be clarified at the start and they need to be collected before the end of the workshop. Even so, a steady trickle goes missing, the most surprising people being among the offenders.

Ideally, the workshop should end with a short time of prayer, or formal worship such as morning or evening prayer, or the Eucharist. Even better, the participants can be encouraged to compose their own liturgy, to make it truly 'the work of the people'. They should be given sufficient time to arrange and decorate the worship space. When allocating different tasks, it is advisable to divide the group into pairs or small teams. One team needs to take responsibility for overseeing the organization and content of the whole time of worship.

Images that have been used by the group can provide a focus for meditation, prayer and celebration by being laid out on the floor in the shape of a cross, star or circle. Resource material should be made available, such as Bibles, prayer manuals, printed liturgies (for all seasons and from around the world), candles, incense, posters, drapery, paper and felt-tip pens. Flowers, branches, stones, water, shells, etc. can be gathered outside where possible. Symbolic artefacts of urban living might be more significant in an inner-city setting. Appropriate music (recorded or live), chanting, drama and liturgical or circle dancing all help to enhance the sensory experience of a worshipping fellowship.

The basic exercise can be followed by a variety of other exercises either on the same day, over a weekend retreat, or on another occasion. Suggestions for follow-up exercises for a variety of purposes are given at the end of each chapter. Courses using images can be offered during different liturgical seasons as in Lent, Holy Week, Ascensiontide or Advent; or as a focus for local and world mission, or a training exercise in evangelism. The options are endless.

Images, idols and icons

The assumption is often made that images of Christ work best in a non-literate, non-book culture. Indeed, they are of great value in such a context as they free people up from being inhibited about low self-worth or lack of formal education. No special requirements or qualifications are needed. Everybody starts in the same place. However, working with images may be even more beneficial in a highly cerebral culture where the left side of the brain is dominant: where rationality and logic take precedence over feeling and emotion, analytical thinking over intuition and imagination, and where people have become alienated from their symbolic inner worlds.

In the first workshop I ever led, I was somewhat taken aback when half-way through a woman burst into tears. She seemed the least likely person to show her feelings in this way, and I was totally unprepared for such a conspicuous display of emotion. It transpired that the woman's elderly and much-loved Golden Labrador dog was dying. The images opened her up to confront her impending sense of loss, allowing her to express a grief that might otherwise have remained locked inside her. The woman's pain was agonizingly real and needed to be addressed.

It was a salutary experience in that it alerted me to the emotional power of the images and the need to respect widely differing responses, to be ready for the unexpected. In fact, the rich variety of people's reactions to the pictures is a never-ending wonder. No two workshops are ever the same and I am continually surprised by people's imaginative insights and the theological depths of people who have had no formal religious training. Truly, this must be the work of the Holy Spirit.

Images of Christ are visual iconic representations of the incarnation, endowed with colour, shape, contour and movement, and embedded in a story, the gospel story of Jesus. By disengaging Christ from his own specific historical and geographical context, the images allow people to meet him in their very own situation, whatever that may be and whoever they are. At the same time, one has to be aware that some people take issue with the way we use such images.

Some Christians feel that because we have no proper revelatory data on which to base a portrayal of Christ, and since every impression and every thought of Jesus should evoke worship, we cannot worship something grounded in sentiment or the imagination. Accordingly, pictures of Christ are in principle a violation of the second commandment, which forbids bowing down to an image or a likeness 'of anything in heaven, or that is on the earth beneath, or that is in the water under the earth' (Exodus 20.4-5). Any use of imagery, therefore, would be tantamount to worshipping graven images and indulging in idolatry. For them, Scripture is the only revelation, the only medium of communication of the mystery of Christ. The incarnate Word and the written word are seen as correlated.[2]

Others disagree. For example, they suggest that while much has been made of the empty cross in Protestant theology, it can itself become an idol which can work against the meaning of the incarnation: 'The empty cross in and of itself does not speak of resurrection. Protestants *interpret* the empty cross as connecting resurrection and crucifixion.'[3]

When I was invited to lead a workshop in a Presbyterian church in Oxford, some people were understandably hesitant about working with images of Christ. But after being reminded of the large picture of Christ the Good Shepherd in the vestry, they relaxed. However, in Wales, a combined workshop of different denominations nearly came unstuck when some members raised serious theological problems about imagery. After a lively discussion we agreed to disagree and continued with the exercise. But a number of people chose pictures of Christ cleansing the Temple, and it didn't take much imagination to get their message.

A distinction must be made between images in a collection like mine and icons in the Orthodox Church. For Orthodox believers, the Christian image is thought to be an extension of the divine incarnation. Icons are thus seen to possess an inherent sacred quality. Since the first century they have been used both as objects of worship and as a means of instruction. In earlier times, the large majority of people were illiterate and relied on wall paintings in their churches to learn about their faith. Vestiges of this tradition remain in ancient cathedrals and churches throughout Europe and Britain. Gruesome paintings of the Doom were a popular theme, designed to instil the fear of God among sinners and reinforce the control of the Church. The crucifixion was another favourite subject, flanked by the Ten Commandments.

For Orthodox Christians, the meaning and content of iconography is as much a subject of theology as biblical study. Icons are not illustrative art. Rather, the symbolic language of their imagery corresponds directly with the contents of Scripture, as do the liturgical texts.[4] Thus, in an Orthodox church, word and image carry equal weight in the preaching of the gospel, evident in the central position of the iconostasis, the screen dividing the nave from the sanctuary. As sacred images, icons are believed to mediate between the sacred and profane worlds. Viewing an icon is viewing God himself. Touching an icon is touching God. It is an exercise which needs to be conducted carefully by a trained *staretz* or spiritual leader.

As sacred art, the painting of an icon, on enamel, metal, mosaic or wooden panels, is rigorously controlled by tradition. The iconographer must ideally be filled with prayer and lead a holy life, and the sacred canon dictates faithfulness to historic original, limited themes, and to specific rules of composition and technique. This includes the preparation of materials and colours, geometry and perspective, gesture and facial features, clothing and symbolic stylization.[5] Any deviation is thought to diminish the religious content of the icon for its beauty is not as an object, but in the divine likeness which it represents. Its role is not to bring us closer to the natural world, but rather to allow us to enter into the sacred realm, inviting us 'into the stillness of contemplating heavenly realities'.[6]

Quite clearly, images of Christ are not objects of adoration or veneration. We see them as secular religious art: simple, down-to-earth pictorial representations of Christ without any pretensions to an innate, divine or mystical aura. Whereas icons are in themselves *of* the divine substance, images are a medium *to* the divine; and while one meditates *on* an icon, one meditates *with* and *through* an image. Through the images we are confronted with Christ, who is always with us, sharing in our journey and inviting us to explore new ways of being his disciples.

As a tool for 'doing theology', the images provide a means to reflect on our faith in the incarnation through art rather than through the written or spoken word. In western practice, we are accustomed to making use of reference books and relying on scholarly expertise. In other parts of the world a populist oral theology is normative, being expressed through extempore prayer, praise, preaching and witnessing. What the images offer is an innovative third alternative in 'doing' theology. This could be an important contribution in initiating 'fresh expressions of church'.[7]

Fresh expressions of church with images

One of the defining marks of contemporary culture, which has profound implications for how we present the gospel, is that we now live in an audio-visual age. We are constantly bombarded by competing images and the world around us reverberates with a cacophony of sound. From advertising, the internet, mobile phones, cinema, television or shopping malls, 'the medium is the message'. In this postmodern context, feeling is more likely to take precedence over thought, the subjective over the objective. For the western Church, this means that the post-Reformation and post-Enlightenment religion of the word is hopelessly out of sync with the audio-visual reality of contemporary life. No wonder that a church which relies on a cerebral exposition of the gospel finds itself increasingly irrelevant and redundant.

People who are seeking a living faith are more likely to respond to a presentation which incorporates the imaginable, intuitional, emotional, relational, and numinous aspects of life, than the propositional and rational alone, if at all.[8] In seeking fresh expressions of church, we should concentrate less on verbalizing our Christian beliefs, and focus more on how we can experience and communicate them through imagery, symbol, art, music, song, drama, dance and story.

Alternative worship communities paved the way in trying to meet this need. From the early 1990s young adults have been attracted by the creative use of multi-media resources in such churches, in a way that involves participants in worship that resonates with popular culture. Imaginative use is made of ritual, symbol and multi-sensory stimuli. Unfortunately, such communities have been too few in number to make much impact on the wider Church. Moreover, the sophisticated technological skills and resources needed are beyond the reach of most congrergations.

In contrast, the more enthusiastic and emotive charismatic worship, or the mystical sensory stimuli experienced in well-presented Catholic devotions, are more widely available. But again, although they may draw in a modest cross-section of devotees, both young and old, the scale is too small, the outreach too limited, and the content too churchy to touch the large majority of seekers, for whom organized religion has no meaning in this post-modern age.

In his seminal work on the challenge of the New Age to the contemporary Church, the Scottish theologian, John Drane, is highly critical of the Church's inability to attract people who are more intuitive and artistic. He grieves that while it continues to ignore or marginalize the riches of its spiritual tradition, New Age movements have been quick to make creative use of this ancient legacy of 'interactive and affective (essentially non-cognitive) spirituality'. Drane believes that hands-on experience is a crucial new dimension of mission:

> There is a need for spiritual disciplines, techniques and practices that will facilitate people in relating to their own inner selves, while consciously and deliberately opening their lives to God's presence, in order to effect radical change ...

People need something tangible through which to express their deepest life commitments. But in order to explore them effectively, they need safe spaces. The creation of such spaces should be a top priority of the church – not only because it will assist the contextualization of the Gospel in contemporary culture, but also because it is a way of being that is quite fundamental and central to the teaching of the New Testament.[9]

Experiential work with images of Christ is a significant way of giving people the unfettered luxury of space and time to try to fathom what the Christian faith means to them. At the same time, they are spiritually nourished as they encounter Christ in other cultures and contexts. In seeking to create a mission-shaped church, there is also the need to respond to the fluidity of contemporary culture by moving away from a static model of church, defined by congregation and buildings, to one in which relationships, networks and communication provide the organizing principles.[10] Because working with images is invariably a group exercise, relationships are integral to the experience. Moreover, the communal context is at the heart of how we relate to Christ and how he relates to us. By using the exercises to express our corporate life in Christ, we begin to experience the pulsating dynamic of a community of faith under the lordship of the living God.

Unlike the Church, such a faith community remains flexible, evolving as it responds to ever-changing needs and situations. This has been the case of a fellowship of which I have been a part in my home village of McGregor, South Africa. Through the regular meeting together of a small group of people at Temenos, a retreat centre in the village, to work with images of Christ, we were in fact exploring 'a new way of being church', although the members would have rejected such a designation. There were no insiders or outsiders in the group and the faith dimension was entirely open-ended. What kept us together was a commitment to explore the meaning of Christ in our lives by tapping into the multi-dimensional diversity incarnate in the images.

Temenos is the Greek word for 'sacred space' and in ancient times it denoted a temple set aside for the healing of body, mind and spirit. The Temenos Retreat Centre is open to all faiths and none. For the last eight years, a twice-daily group meditation has taken place either in The Little Way, a Celtic chapel set in a garden beside a duck pond, or The Well, a non-sectarian sanctuary lit only by candles and with a bubbling fountain. In the chapel there is a life-size mural of Jesus and the Buddha embracing each other, encapsulating the catholic spirit of Temenos, as well as icons of Jesus and Mary. Meditation lasts for 20 minutes, and the village is continually refreshed by the spiritual heart which beats in its midst.

The Centre boasts a Zen Garden, a Sufi shrine or *tempietta*, two meditation cells, an open-air altar to Mother Mary, a statue of a dancing St Teresa of Avila, patron saint of Temenos, a spiral walk with symbols of world religions set in a stone circle, a healing garden with treatment rooms, and a well-stocked library. A small Anglican fellowship holds weekly Evensong in the chapel as well as a monthly Eucharist; but the festivals and feast days of different world religions have also been regularly celebrated. There is also a short, lay-led act of worship in the chapel on Sunday mornings.

A two-hour drive from Cape Town, the nineteenth-century village of McGregor is situated in the Breede River Winelands region, on the edge of semi-desert known as the Little Karroo. The original Afrikaans-speaking farming community derives its living from apricots, olives and vines, and is served by the Dutch Reformed Church. Tucked away in a valley at the end of 'a road going nowhere', McGregor has attracted a growing number of artists, potters, musicians, writers, healers of every description, New Age seekers, and similar people. The majority in this cosmopolitan settlement are retired. A few still attend church with varying degrees of regularity, but most severed any formal ties many years ago. Some have been deeply hurt by the Church, others have become disenchanted with what it has to offer but have not lost their faith. It is from a cross-section of this constituency, together with the Temenos leadership, that we drew a regular group of 10-15 people who met fortnightly to work with the pictures.

The core members of the group had all had some former denominational connection be this Roman Catholic, Anglican, Methodist or Reformed, with a handful retaining an affiliation. The rest would probably describe themselves as fringe or lapsed Christians, anthroposophists, pagans, agnostics, or just spiritually curious, with a penchant for eastern traditions. Unusually, the sexes remained evenly divided with three couples among the regulars. Our only black member was an Anglican priest from a Brahmin Hindu background in Bombay, but with worldwide pastoral experience and western theological expertise. All were unconditionally welcome to the fellowship and because Temenos attracts a rich variety of characters from many countries, we were constantly challenged by the insights of visitors. These included two women of Jewish extraction, a Tibetan and a Zen Buddhist, a Sufi, a born-again Christian, agnostics, a variety of New Agers, and a Findhorn community member from Scotland.

We met in the Temenos restaurant, seated round a fire in winter and on the verandah in the summer heat, but always in a circle. The setting reinforced the non-sectarian nature of the meeting and made for a relaxed, inclusive and non-judgemental atmosphere. The choice of theme was generally set by the leader, but was open to people's particular interests as well as following the Christian liturgical year. No money was ever involved. Temenos generously provided the venue, this type of communal gathering being very much at the heart of the Centre's vision.

After welcoming visitors at the beginning of each meeting, the evening's theme was introduced followed by an appropriate Scripture reading and a short theological exposition, if that seemed helpful. Often it is better to let people work without any pre-emptive theological input, and to offer teaching at the end. People seemed to welcome a biblical exegesis if it was given in a user-friendly manner. The fact that the exercise was lay-led did not mean that we dispensed with theology.

Depending on the theme, we either had a mixed display of images or a number of packs relating to the subject. Occasionally we worked with only one or two images so that we could compare insights. Sometimes we worked singly, or in twos and threes. It is good to change the format so that people do not become bored. Normally a question was set at the start relating to the theme, such as 'Who is Christ for you in this particular situation?' or, 'How do you identify with the people involved in this gospel story? How does this relate to your life?

The honesty, profundity and radical nature of the theology that emerged continued to amaze us. A remarkably high level of trust developed over time, that freed people to share both their joy and pain, laughter and tears. Working over an extended period also allowed the group to grow in their depth of understanding. For example, an experienced Jungian analyst highlighted the shadow side of Christ in an image. He encouraged us to acknowledge the repressed, hidden side of ourselves, bring it to the surface and integrate it so that as people we might become whole. Artists focused our attention on the nuances of their craft and historical details that would have escaped our attention, while naturalists awakened our senses to the God of creation. Non-Christian friends helped us to see the gospel story with new eyes and to be wary of making assumptions.

Each session lasted about an hour and a quarter and was followed by a meal of soup and bread, with local wine flowing freely. We took turns in providing home-cooked food and drinks. Discussion was seldom theological but the fact of having done theology together, and of having shared at depth, meant that conversation was always warm and personal. Reciprocity was a consistent factor in the impromptu counselling and comforting of each other as past griefs and present anxieties surfaced. At the same time, much of the meal was punctuated with laughter and this happy togetherness continued into our village life.

The sharing of bread and wine in the meal represented the sacramental dimension – a true *agape* fellowship. By now, the mood was so richly endowed with warmth that a formal grace would have been gratuitous. The feasting was not an extra but an inalienable part of the whole experience. The sharing of food has always been considered sacramental in indigenous traditions throughout the world and in other religions. The Wedding at Cana exercise was celebrated with champagne and special delicacies prepared by one of our members who was a chef. Regulars spoke of the enrichment of meeting and eating together, more especially as it involved a cross-section of people who would not normally have socialized together.

For most of the group, the initial reaction to the images was one of surprise: surprise at being confronted by a multi-cultural Christ, surprise at the differences in people's responses and the originality of our discussions, and surprise at the effectiveness of this way of working. Perhaps the greatest surprise was the emotional power of the images. Said one, a trained counsellor working with children:

> The visual impact is so powerful that you can get in touch with your feelings just by looking, and being given time to take it all in. The images go straight to the heart. You are seeing instead of listening to someone talking or reading, so that your mind doesn't get in the way. It helps that comments are only needed at a later stage and that you don't have to justify your choice of picture, just let it speak to you. The images are very personal and made me feel very emotional, especially those that had anything to do with children or were about love. People, especially the older generation, are generally frightened of going internally and try avoiding it. But the power of the visual makes it easier to get that deep connection.

This friend was particularly struck by the therapeutic potential of the images, and I actually had the opportunity of working with one of the group on her own as she sought a new direction in her life. We started with a fairly general selection of pictures and then she gradually whittled them down to six. What surprised me as the process unfolded, was how her chosen pictures came together thematically around brokenness, healing and celebration.

Another friend, a potter, saw the images as a wonderful way of learning because of their ability to involve people who were shy or diffident about sharing something of themselves. Obviously some people do get stuck, locked in by their inhibitions. But what impressed her most was 'the hidden way' in which the images called out an emotional response:

Why I chose the picture, why it spoke to me, told me a lot about myself. It was also fascinating listening to how pictures around the same theme, or even identical pictures, talked to different people. We were a varied group and quite unselfconsciously they communicated much about who they were and how they thought. I also loved the way the images portrayed Christ in a new light, the new insights this gave me. The pictures freshened the whole story of Jesus because they were so different, bringing it all alive. The black images in particular gave me a whole new and unexpected perspective.

One picture that has remained with her was of the Last Supper. It was set in a market place with crowds standing around an inn. She recalls:

It was all so human. The pictures tell us so much about the human condition. The emphasis put on religion is so often divorced from the everyday things of life. Too often the Church tries to contain and grab the story to itself. Dogma closes people off and they opt out rather than confront it. But the Jesus story is so universal. It speaks to anyone, whoever and wherever they might be.

This friend has an Anglican school background but sees herself as an agnostic who is struggling to fathom the mystery of life.

Contemporary writers talk about the power of stories to break through people's defences: to open them up to new ways of thinking and being, to encourage them to share in both the suffering and pain and the joy and celebration of others, and to motivate them to become actively involved in challenging new situations. The images take this a step further in that they enable people to enter into a dialogue between their personal stories and the gospel story: to start integrating their lived experience with their experience of God and so make sense of who they are and what they are called to be as 'followers of the Way'.

As a model for a new ecclesia, the Wednesday group at Temenos was a place to belong and to feel at home spiritually regardless of one's background. The fortnightly gathering prided itself on being ecumenical, multireligious, multinational, gender equal, lay-led and non-hierarchical. The images, supported by Scripture readings and theological reflection, constituted the defining framework of the fellowship. All the ubiquitous signatures of a typical church service such as prayer, sermon, singing, creed, confession and absolution, and the clutter of service and hymn books, were refreshingly absent. Instead, people who would not normally have given Christ a thought found themselves inspired by the images to engage with the reality of Christ. The group no longer meets but the flexibility of the resource means that new directions are always possible.

✳ ✳ ✳ ✳ ✳

Exercises using images of Christ

The first set of exercises are designed to follow on from the basic exercise. They are quite straightforward and particularly useful in opening up discussion in a plenary session. They are also ideal for any sort of house group, a PCC or Church Council, Mothers' Union meeting, chaplaincy work (in prison, schools, tertiary education), confirmation classes for both adults and young people, all-age groups or children's groups.

1. Identifying factors which influenced our selection of images

- How many people tried to find a picture of Jesus as he might have looked in Palestine in the first century? Was this unimportant for others?

- How many chose a picture because it emphasized some aspect of Jesus' earthly ministry, such as healing and teaching? Why?

- How many chose a white Jesus? Or specifically chose a picture showing Jesus incarnated in another culture? Why?

- How many chose an image of Jesus suffering? Why?

- How many chose an image of the risen and ascended Christ? Why?

- How many chose an abstract image of Christ rather than a portrait? Why?

- How many preferred a symbolic image or simply words rather than a picture? Why?

- Does it matter that people envisage Jesus in different ways?[11]

2. Critiquing images of Christ

Which images did you not like, or had problems with, and why?

- This is a good way of helping people to express their views and, in clarifying who Christ is for them, identifying what they find difficult.

- A critique may be based on what is perceived as poor or tasteless art, simplistic or sentimental imagery, or unedifying representations of Christ. But be aware that what is distasteful to some may well resonate with others. Remember too that profound theological statements can arise from the most unpromising pictures.

- There may be racial criticisms: many people have problems with a black, brown or yellow Christ, even those who are not themselves Caucasian. Similarly, there may be cultural criticisms in seeing Christ depicted as Asian, African or Latin American.

- Others may have social, political or religious concerns which need drawing out and discussing. Some people cannot envisage an angry Christ, or Christ incarnate in horrific or unfamiliar situations such as war, prison, as an AIDS sufferer, smoking a cigarette, or as a football player.

- Theological concerns about people's differing views concerning the representation of Christ will need to be discussed.

3. Images that challenge

Choose an image which is problematical for you but which could enlarge or enrich your understanding of Christ.

- After meditating on the images, explore the nature of this challenge in pairs or small groups.

- Reasons for the challenge may vary considerably. Is it because the picture is too modern or outdated, too anthropomorphic or too abstract, from a different culture or situation to one's own, or depicts Christ with a different skin colour, as female, laughing, angry, tortured, as a refugee, dancing, etc.?

4. Using contrasting images

A pair of contrasting images is used to enable the group to do its own theology.

The Laughing Christ from Canada and *The Angry Christ* from the Philippines are a good example. See the case study in chapter 3, 'Action stations with images', page 59, where they were used to enable a church youth group to identify ethical issues and motivate them to action.

- The facilitator needs to provide
  * information about the images
  * leading questions to draw out discussion
  * Bibles for theological reflection with suitable references
  * time for meditation and prayer
  * planning for any action that might arise from the discussion.

5. Using a limited number of images

Between five and ten contrasting images are fixed at strategic points around the room. Walls or display panels are best.

- After a brief introduction, people are asked to walk round the display and spend time looking at the images. They are then invited to stand by the image of their choice.

- Time is given for each group to share their reasons for choosing their image. If people find they are by themselves in front of an image, they could team up and discuss their respective choices, or they could share their thoughts with the leader.

- Group discussion follows to allow reflection on the choices made:
  * What images were most popular and why?
  * What images attracted little interest and why?
  * What images were completely ignored and why?
  * What are the christological implications of the choices made?
  * Can the group discern any sense of a corporate spirituality, e.g. a loving protective Christ, a Christ who challenges, a suffering Christ, etc.?
  * What other images of Christ were relevant?

6. Using Christmas cards

Christmas cards are a readily available resource with which to explore the nature of the annunciation and the nativity. Ask people to collect and bring a variety of cards, historical and contemporary, and from different parts of the world. These should include the sentimental and the kitsch. Set them out on display. Pictures of the annunciation can be separated from the nativity if they are to be dealt with in separate discussions.

- As an icebreaker allow the group to reflect on the variety of cards and explore their response to them.

- Choose an image and meditate on it. Share in pairs, small groups, or as a larger group the reasons for your choice.

- Have images from different cultures and contexts played a part in your choices? Discuss.

- Use the cards to explore the role of different characters in the stories – the Archangel Gabriel and Mary, Mary and Elizabeth, Joseph and Mary, the angels and the shepherds, the wise men, the Christ child, onlookers at the nativity. Working with the relevant Bible passages is recommended. For this exercise they are Matthew 1.18–2.11; Luke 1.26-38 (annunciation); 1.39-45 (visitation); 2.1-21 (nativity).

- Using images of the annunciation, explore the role of Mary as the first missionary. Read the Magnificat (Luke 1.46-55).

- Which images would be selected to reach people with the Christmas message who have little or no understanding of the biblical story of Christmas?

- What do the different portrayals of the nativity from over the ages and from around the world tell us about changes in our understanding of Christ's birth?

- Appropriate readings or drama can be used together with the images to bring the nativity story alive.

- Discuss the cards themselves, exploring the commercial and secular aspects. How does the group respond to the 'Put Christ back into Christmas' call from many church people?

- What does the group think of the images used in church advertising over Christmas, especially the more challenging ones?

7. Images of Christ in our church

Walk round your church building and list all the images of Christ you can find.

- This exercise can be done in pairs, the idea being to see who can compile the longest list. You need to look in detail so that you can recall the images later. Rough sketches can be an aid to memory.

- Images can be symbolic or representational and can include statues, stained-glass windows, crosses and crucifixes, banners, biblical texts, Sunday school drawings, images on lecterns and pulpits, paintings, a reredos, carvings on altars and altar frontals, kneelers, memorials, etc.

- After a set time the group comes together to share their lists, and reflect on the Christology visibly present in the church.
  - * What impact might this have on worshippers?
  - * What impact might this have on visitors?
- Discussion can include the provision of information about the various images as well as teaching about them. It might even lead to the compilation of a study guide.
- This is a particularly good exercise with children and young people in Sunday school or in confirmation preparation, or with a group of adult catechumens.
- In order to raise awareness, regular worshippers can be asked to recall as many images of Christ in the church as they can before starting the exercise.

2

Faith Taking Flesh

Incarnating Christ in north-east England

In the north-east I found a popular culture specific to the region, and, working with images of Christ, I discovered a Christian faith that was uniquely rooted in the local context and culture. Over the centuries the people have incarnated Christ into their everyday experience, interpreting the gospel independently of the Church in order to make sense of their lives. Their ancient Celtic heritage, folk religion and Geordie savvy have all played their part, as have economic and social deprivation, class factors and the impact of postmodernity on the north-eastern way of life.

So, for example, a farmer in the Wear Valley drew on his own experience with cattle to identify Christ as the Good Stockman rather than Shepherd. He described how, in order to get recalcitrant cattle to pass through a gate to fresh pastures, he would have to go down on all fours and crawl slowly through the muck and the mire. The cattle, being curious, would gather round and follow him. In a similar way, Christ had to suffer death on the cross in order to rescue us and lead us to God. For the stockman, the cross is the

gateway to heaven and, like the cattle, we are called to follow Christ through the cross (John 10.27-28). This analogy gave the stockman strength to persevere through all the many difficulties of his rural life, including foot and mouth disease.

The same farmer told another story about Christ the Good Stockman, which epitomizes northern humour. A priest battled his way through a snowstorm to take a service at a remote church, only to find a lone stockman awaiting him. The priest was all for going straight home; but the stockman argued that even when the weather was this bad, he would still go out on the hill to feed his heifers, no matter if only one turned up. The priest got the message and thought, that, in that case he would give him the full works – four hymns, long prayers, and an even longer sermon. When at the end the stockman was asked if he was satisfied, he replied, 'When only one heifer comes for hay, I don't give her the whole load.' Such is rural wisdom.

Christ the Good Shepherd is a favourite image in the north-east, and so is Christ depicted with animals and children. This imagery is illustrated in the stained-glass of the many Victorian churches built during the coal-mining era. The Gentle Jesus paintings of Margaret Tarrant (1888-1959) provided the template and remain extraordinarily popular. Tarrant's Jesus is the sinless one, who identifies with the vulnerable and innocent, and is incarnated in the peace and tranquility of an idealized English countryside. This may seem overly sentimental but it is a spirituality that speaks to a poverty-stricken and excluded people of a loving, caring Christ who wraps his arms around them and protects them in times of trouble. There is even a miner's banner featuring Christ with children, and the text: 'Suffer Little Children to Come Unto Me' (Mark 10.14). This is in contrast to other such banners bearing Trade Union, or political images and slogans.

For northern women, survival and escapism have been the historical, conditioned responses to lives of poverty and hardship. Moreover, although family patterns have changed to include many variations of 'family', traditional extended family ties, with their strong matriarchal lineages and love of children, remain firm. Tarrant's painting of the Loving Shepherd offers a fatherly sense of security and protection against a menacing world, especially in situations when real-life fathers fall short of expectations. This theme surfaced regularly in workshops, often accompanied by tears.

In the northern context, God is seen as 'looking after us and all other people in the world, like a good shepherd looks after his sheep. He gives us what we need and shows us what to do.' The laity tend to see their role as 'lost sheep', while the clergy are regarded as 'good shepherds'. A priest's wife tells of a young mother, burdened with family and health problems, who was overwhelmed by a home visit from the vicar: 'Like all of us, she was longing for the Good Shepherd to come and find her. The vicar's visit was one little ray of hope and perhaps the start of her realizing that God really is seeking for her and longing to provide the purpose her life needs.'

However, this model of ministry raises certain difficulties. It encourages a male-dominated image of God, reinforced by the authoritarian role of some clergy, with a dependent laity. At a parish weekend in which images were used to explore new directions in mission, the priest chose the Loving Shepherd. The image failed to inspire the visionary leadership needed to bring about longed-for change. The more challenging aspects of the gospel are totally overshadowed by the nurturing element in this image, however urgent the pastoral concerns. In contrast, poor people in the southern hemisphere have themselves taken responsibility for their lives and become actively involved in following a liberator Christ.

In the communities of the north-east, once based on coal-mining, another popular image is Holman Hunt's *The Light of the World*, first exhibited in 1854 (cf. John 8.12, 9.5, 12.46). Stained-glass reproductions of this painting are found in a number of Durham churches, while prints grace innumerable homes. Undoubtedly, a nostalgic spirituality lingers on, harking back to supposedly happier times past. However, the picture still offers a theological challenge: a bearded Jesus who, clothed in shining white and patiently knocking at a door, is in reality knocking at the door of our hearts, inviting us to repent and let him in. The overgrown garden in the painting, and the brambles obstructing Christ's way, symbolize all that makes for personal sin, selfish greed and worldliness. Without a handle to the door, this gentle Jesus, who looks straight into our hearts, must wait for us to admit him into our lives (cf. Matthew 7.7). But while the evangelistic message, reinforced by countless sermons, is soon trotted out, it is the symbolism of the glowing lamp held by Christ that has been contextualized in local north-eastern theology: 'It's like a miner's lamp, see.'

In the past, Durham was a well-known mining area. Although the pits no longer exist, former pit villages remain dotted around the county and mining still defines the life experience, and permeates the faith, of older people. Images of miners' lamps adorn both Mothers' Union and Trade Union banners, lamps feature in stained-glass windows and church memorials, and, in some village churches, a permanently lit lamp stands on an altar or hangs next to an aumbry holding the reserved sacrament. Not surprisingly, Christ the Light of the World symbolizes hope. People believe that the light of Christ will overcome darkness, just as the miners' lamps did deep down in the pits, and that our Lord and Saviour will lead them safely through the many vicissitudes of life, as he protected the miners in their daily toil.

Coal-mining was dangerous work and the mining community looked to the church for support. A miner's widow recalls that in her village one had to be early to get a seat for Evensong, this after two Communion services and Matins in the morning. According to her, the church sustained the miners by bringing them closer to God, giving them the strength to face the ever-present perils of their work underground. Although former miners are not renowned for articulating their faith, they knew how to live it.

Reports of mining disasters contain emotional accounts of entombed men scratching their testimonies on any material that came to hand. Miners who survived an explosion knew that, trapped by a rock fall, they stood little chance of being rescued. The messages they left spoke of deep religious convictions. As they awaited death in the dark, the 'marras' would pray together, their mutual dependence underground having forged bonds of brotherhood which gave them courage to endure. After the Seaham Colliery disaster in 1880, a beam was uncovered with the chalk-inscribed words: 'The Lord has been with us, we are all ready for heaven. Ric Cole, ½ past 2 O'Clock Thursday'; and 'Bless the Lord, we have had a godly Prayer meeting, every man ready for glory. Praise the Lord.' The beam now has pride of place in New Seaham Christ Church, next to the former pit.

A visiting Indian priest offered us a challenging image of Christ the Coal-Miner, using as his text the tradition of 'the harrowing of hell' (Revelation 1.18, 9.1, 20.1, cf. the Apostles' Creed). In the incarnation, Christ came down to earth. But after the crucifixion Christ descended into hell (Anastasis), symbolizing his conquest over evil and death, and bringing hope to both the living and the dead. In the harrowing of hell, Christ battled with the powers of darkness and emerged victorious. While the mines may have closed, the unemployed and marginalized of society can still feel trapped by poverty and despair. A Catholic nun, working in a deprived community, tells of a destitute young woman who is confident of going to heaven when she dies because she has already experienced so much hell here on earth.

The poor do not share the earth with the 'haves'; they are the 'have-nots'. This is where Christ steps in to suffer with them. The good news is that Christ triumphs over the powers of every sort of hell. This is the hope offered by the ascension: hope of being rescued from captivity and darkness, from being out of sight, discarded and forgotten. The paradigm of being trapped into a subterranean space recurs repeatedly in the Scriptures. The harrowing of hell becomes a story of solidarity and liberation from a seemingly desperate situation. It is a spirituality of being with Christ, and Christ being with us. No wonder that images of Christ in industrial wastelands, redundant dockyards, smoking rubbish dumps, urban ghettoes and shanty towns resonate with those living in tough situations. They take courage that Christ is with them.

But all is not doom and gloom. The *Laughing Christ, Jesus Christ – Liberator*, painted by the Canadian artist, Willis S. Wheatley (*The Christ We Share*, no. 1), is another popular picture in workshops. People note that, whereas Christ is generally depicted as soulful and serious, this image radiates joy, and northerners enjoy a laugh. In a Stockton parish, a girl serving in a rather seedy pub chose a quirky contemporary painting by Beryl Cook, said to be 'Britain's most popular painter'. The voluptuous, English Madonna has large, staring eyes, a double chin and red cupid's-bow lips, while the plumply naked Christ child has golden curls, a wicked grin and an in-your-face bare bottom. A blue bird is perched on Christ's finger à la Velazquez. The barmaid later bravely pinned the picture above the bar counter – 'a bit up-market compared to the 1930s' cartoons on the wall'. While her job left little time to talk, and it was hard to compete with the loud music, the image provoked considerable discussion, especially as it was so unlike the holy pictures of Christ the locals had seen in church.

In a Darlington parish, a record was kept of images chosen during an Ash Wednesday workshop. Out of a total of 30, eight had Jesus with animals or children, while another six were of Holman Hunt's *The Light of the World* or the Good Shepherd. Such a tally is typical in the region. The suffering of Christ is another common theme. The seven selected images were a Holocaust Pieta, helping someone to reflect on grief, the tortured Christ from

Brazil (*The Christ We Share*, no. 2), an Asian Dancing Christ, symbolizing release from pain and suffering, the South African Peace Banner, with Christ identifying with the struggle of his suffering people for justice and freedom, a Chagall crucifixion, and two African crucifixions, one made from barbed wire and the other from thorns. Of the two blind people present, one asked for an image contrasting light and dark, while the other wanted a peaceful image, of Jesus washing a disciple's feet. The humanity of Christ featured in five pictures: with an African woman of Samaria, as a Cameroon slave-boy holding up a golden bowl (symbolizing the gift of himself – *The Christ We Share*, no. 13), as a Nicaraguan feeding the multitude, the more familiar Rembrandt head of Christ, and the Beecroft Christ, *The Lord looked upon Peter.* The last two people both chose a contemporary image of the risen Christ in front of the empty tomb with the text 'I am the Resurrection and the life', which they saw as the essence of Christianity.

In the West we are accustomed to anthropologists analyzing the religious beliefs and practices of indigenous peoples in the Third World. But for an English regional community to be subjected to anthropological dissection, and to have its corporate spirituality described in similar terms, came as something of a shock to local clergy. But, as Stephen Conway, now Archdeacon of Durham, looked back on a workshop with members of the Church Council in his former Tees Valley parish, he rightly said:

Why should we be shocked? In fact, it was most helpful to think about the pastoral and caring spirituality of the North East, expressed in favoured images of Christ as gentle Shepherd and the welcomer of children. At first sight, one might think that the fit was odd. After all, the communities of the region have gone through so much hardship that people have had to learn how to be tough and self-reliant through poverty, through hard physical labour and through long-term unemployment. It is precisely this unrelenting environment, however, which draws us to warm and accepting images of the Lord. People know a lot about the Cross in their own experience. Traditionally, communities have been held together by resilient women who have provided mutual support and loyal care. The Lord who is the source of that embrace draws us in. More challenging images can be left over from the struggle of living and loving. The images workshop is also the place, of course, where the assumptions of our spirituality can be reviewed and safely challenged.

This sort of analysis has profound implications for the Church in England because until recently it largely ignored local context and culture in its theological thinking and missiological praxis. Even now it tends to focus on 'exotic' sub-cultures like youth, the arts, pubs and housing estates. No wonder that our precious mission programmes fail to deliver the goods. Too often they are based on sociological assumptions culled from a literate, comfortable, middle-class context, in a one-size-fits-all package, disregarding the lived reality of those in quite different situations. Too often they follow a top-down process which takes no cognizance of creative initiatives struggling to blossom from below, just waiting to be given space and encouragement to grow in the local setting. What is needed is a missionary praxis that critiques both positive and negative aspects of popular culture and beliefs, and gives people the freedom to do their own theology.

One faith, different theologies

Coming from South Africa I have a concern for contextual theology, that is, a theology that arises out of a particular context and addresses the needs and concerns of that context. The Bible is a prime example of a contextual record. God's acts of redemption and liberation are recorded in the events of the Scriptures, long after they supposedly happened and from the different perspectives of those affected or involved in the God-human covenant. The gospel writers are doing contextual theology when they draw on their own unique experiences and memories of Jesus to bring his message alive, but address quite different constituencies in their telling of the same basic story.

Indeed, all theologies are contextual, whether they are acknowledged to be or not, since all theological thinking is determined by the immediate context of those engaged in the doing of theology. However, contextual theology per se implies 'the *conscious* attempt to do theology from within the context of real life in the world'.[1] It is a way of doing theology, a method, and is usually a community effort in that it starts with the experiences and concerns of a specific group of people.

Albert Nolan, Dominican theologian from South Africa, maintains that 'any practising Christian can *do* theology ... all that is necessary is an active faith'.[2] He argues that, 'theology has for too long been an abstract study reserved for academic experts – producing a sytematisation of answers to questions we no longer ask or at most an adaptation of answers to past questions which must now serve as a reservoir for answers to today's questions'.[3] John Pridmore, a Church of England priest in inner-city Hackney, London, would concur. He maintains that 'the only theology that is any use is theology born out of human need, not theology prepared in aseptic isolation and then applied like Elastoplast ... Theology comes to life when it is shaped by what people in Hackney – and Harrogate – actually care about.'[4]

This does not mean that people with scholarly expertise are sidelined. Access to a wide range of resources from both the social scientific disciplines and theology are needed to throw light upon the many questions that will naturally arise. As Nolan explains, different people in different times and places, and in different parts of the world, will ask different questions about faith according to their different historical, socio-economic, political and cultural contexts. Consequently, this will give rise to different theologies. However, 'this does not deny the fact that faith as a commitment to God in Jesus Christ remains the same at all times and in all circumstances. In other words, while there is one faith, there can be different theologies.'[5]

Names given to different theologies around the world reflect the diversity of contexts. There is Liberation Theology in Latin America, Dalit Theology in India, Water Buffalo Theology in Thailand, Jubilee Theology in the Caribbean, Kola Nut Theology in Nigeria, Green and Feminist Theology in the West, Womanist Theology among black women, and African and Black Theology in South Africa. In north-east England there are a number of possible theologies, while in Oxford we had Commuter, Micro-Chip, Oxfam and National Heritage Theologies. But the one that superseded all others I called Duvet Theology. Here, the context was defined by the overarching need for the Church to provide succour and protection in a world which seemed to be spinning out of control, different tog ratings indicating the required levels of comfort.

In workshops, members of the clergy, somewhat nervous of lay incursions into their hitherto well-preserved domain, are prone to ask whether contextual theology is '*good* theology'. The assumption here is that theology must be couched in an academically correct doctrinal format and language by professionally trained experts. But of what use is a doctrinally sophisticated theology if it fails to connect with people's spiritual needs and prevents them from living out their faith in radically different contexts? In working with images we have to be aware of our own assumptions and biases, so deeply immersed in our western theological baggage.

Obviously there is a danger that because we are advocating a grassroots theology that invites people to begin with their own experience, this may lead to a simplistic and uncritical use of the Bible, or even a syncretistic incorporation of folk beliefs. This is where professional theologians sympathetic to the process can help develop the necessary exegetical skills among the laity, and offer the gift of their theological scholarship, without disempowering the people involved.

The work of the Nicaraguan priest, Ernesto Cardenal, among the people of Solentiname during the 1960s and '70s, exemplifies how a people's theology can take shape in the context of exploitation and suffering through an ongoing engagement with the gospel. In *The Gospel in Solentiname*, colourful paintings illustrate the story of how daily Bible studies which Cardenal conducted among the *campesinos* resulted in their becoming politically radicalized and highly motivated to realize a just society through revolutionary action.[6]

The evangelistic ministry of Vincent Donavan among the Masai in East Africa is also well known. His primary concern in taking the gospel to an indigenous people was to respect their culture, not destroy it.[7] In a western context, with a long-established Church, it is just as important to take popular culture seriously, not revile or ignore it. Donavan's work was based on the fundamental question: 'Who is the Christ I preach?' In offering the Masai the unique contribution of Christianity, he tried to pare away all the cultural accretions of western civilization. The western Church, which until recently set the theological agenda for the World Church, now needs to learn to live with, and learn from, the pluralism embedded in the incarnation.

The incarnation is at the heart of contextualization – 'and the Word became flesh and dwelt among us' (John 1.14). This is the *skandalon* of Christology. Christ of first-century Palestine takes flesh and is born anew within each and every tradition and context. As the Lord of history, he embraces all cultures yet transcends them all. During his time on earth Jesus gave his disciples the freedom to speculate on his identity by asking: 'Who do you say I am?' (Matthew 16.13-20; Mark 8.29; Luke 9.18-21). This enigma of the Gospels is not about some convoluted, ontological scrutiny of the mystery of the incarnation. Rather, it liberates us to identify Christ in a myriad forms and guises. Christ's question to his disciples may be paraphrased as: 'How do you see me? In what context?' Even Paul's conversion on the road to Damascus was initiated by his posing the question: 'Who are you, Lord?' (Acts 9.5). The range of possible responses regarding Jesus' identity is as wide as the range of people who are confronted by it. There are indeed as many theologies and Christologies as there are Christian traditions.

Notwithstanding this manifold diversity in responding to the incarnation, our faith is rooted in the irreducible humanity of the unseen, invisible God who has taken on flesh in Jesus. This God entered into our history. In Jesus, he shared our joys and sorrows, suffered, died and rose again from the dead. Christ, the incarnate Son, is the visible image through whom we seek God the Father, who is beyond all images. We, too, are incarnate beings, made like Jesus in the image of God. But while Jesus is the true image of God, we are only incomplete images.

As incomplete images, we find in the portrayals of Christ a powerful means of communing indirectly with God. Each image is a window, a channel to the ongoing process of incarnation. Through meditating on an image, Christ's love becomes incarnate, visible, touchable, feelable, in all the great contextual variety of creation eternally incarnate in diverse situations and traditions.

So, for example, the Via Dolorosa can be traced in all the innumerable struggles for justice in world history. The resurrection happened in the Holy Sepulchre in Jerusalem, but recurs wherever the forces of justice, peace and harmony triumph over the principalities and powers of oppression, darkness and chaos. In times of trial, our meditation on an image is a way of inviting Christ to incarnate himself afresh in our own specific context with his reconciling love.

The writer of Hebrews stresses the validity of the incarnation for all time: 'Jesus Christ is the same yesterday, today, and forever' (13.8). The sameness of Jesus, however, ought to be grasped in terms of the tension between the Jesus of history and the Christ of faith. When we meditate with our chosen images of Christ, we are brought face to face with the 'little' incarnation of our faith and thus participate in the mystery of the historic incarnation. A typical image traces this ongoing incarnation, this story of Jesus in a given situation. Without understanding that specific 'little' incarnation, there is no possible comprehension of *the* incarnation. As Meister Eckhart says, 'If Jesus of Nazareth were not to be born again in our hearts today, what use would it be that he was born in Nazareth two thousand years ago?'

An image is not merely a representation of Christ, therefore, but an indispensable revelation of the incarnation. For instance, Jesus the Maori shaman in New Zealand is not just a symbolic embodiment of Christ but a direct presentation of him in that particular situation. In the glass etching of the Maori Christ in the Galilee chapel of St Faith's Church in Ohinemutu, the traditionally robed figure appears to walk on the water of Lake Rotorua, the crater lake seen through the window. For the Maori people, this is not just Christ dressed as a Maori shaman but Christ as he reveals himself to them. He is their very own Jesus.

Similarly, for the Masai in East Africa, a Rembrandt or a Michelangelo, a Salvador Dali or a Stanley Spencer is irrelevant to their specific *Heilsgeschichte*, history of salvation. To them, the only real Christ is the Masai Jesus: The Lion of Judah, portrayed as an African warrior (*The Christ We Share*, no. 6). He is both the elder brother of all humanity and the elder brother of their ancestors, 'the living dead'. Through the incarnation, the particularity of Christ for each culture is brought together with his universality for all people, the images providing the connecting link.

The many faces of Christ in European history

The process of translating the gospel into contemporary cultural forms has been going on since the beginning of the Christian era. The incarnation itself can be seen as an act of translation, the Word of God translated into the flesh of Christ within a particular social reality. This translation process was then extended through the contextualizing of Christ's teaching in four quite different Gospels. Subsequently, the 'infinite translatability' of Christianity meant that as it expanded ever further, it was able to both transform and to be transformed by the receiving culture.[8] Moreover, it was the people themselves, not the Church, who took the initiative in drawing on indigenous thought-patterns, imagery and symbolism to establish vernacular expressions of their new-found faith and to relate it to their everyday experience.

Each era in Christian history, such as Hellenistic-Roman or postmodern, has produced new themes, determined by specific points of reference in a cultural area and dependent on language, history, culture and geographical location. Because the translation of Christianity is an ongoing process, expressions of the faith will continue to take new forms. At the present time, the heart of Christianity has shifted from its ancient power base in Europe to the southern hemisphere, and Africa now takes centre-stage. Indeed, Christianity must continue to be translated, must go on entering local cultures everywhere – whether these are youth, inner-city, housing estate, multiracial, regional or rural – and interact with them, or else it will wither and die.[9]

In the translation process itself, *inculturation* is the term commonly used to describe the symbolic exchange which takes place in the ongoing dialogue between the form in which the Christian faith is presented and the receiving culture.[10] In a historical survey of the spread of Christianity across Europe, the Dutch missiologist, Anton Wessels, has examined the inculturation of the gospel in the Graeco-Roman, Celtic and Germanic contexts. He shows how the new elements in the gospel teaching interacted with symbols, images and myths of the vernacular culture in each age and place to become incarnated as indigenous expressions of Christianity.[11]

According to Wessels, if the old indigenous religions were weak they eventually disappeared. If they were popular and deeply entrenched in the symbolic world of the receiving culture, significant elements of the old were co-opted and transformed by the incoming culture of the Church. The success of this cross-cultural diffusion of Christian faith depended on how firmly the new became rooted in the imagery, symbols, language, concepts, customs and traditions of the old. Significant, too, was the extent to which Christianity was perceived as adding new value to the symbolic world of the vernacular culture to meet new contextual needs.[12] This process remains true today as much in Britain, Europe and North America as in Africa, Asia and Latin America.

Symbolic images of Christ date back to the first century. Tertullian refers to representations of the Good Shepherd on chalices, while, in the fourth century, Eusebius of Caesarea records the existence of a number of portraits of Christ, of which he disapproved, together with other biblical figures. But these ancient images did not survive, destroyed either by the iconoclastic onslaught or the wear and tear of time.[13]

The oldest extant images of Christ the Good Shepherd are found in Rome, in catacomb murals, on sarcophagi and grave slabs, and as an ivory statuette, dating from the third century on. These portrayals represent Christ as a slender, beardless young man either surrounded by sheep or carrying a sheep on his shoulder.[14] Although this early Christian motif has strong New Testament resonances (John 10.14-15; Matthew 15.24), the Graeco-Roman iconography is not initially Christian in origin. It draws its symbolic power of deliverance from the classical image of Hermes, protector of flocks, carrying a ram in his arms. This popular imagery, also present in Etruscan art, was then co-opted and reinterpreted by early Christians to symbolize Christ as the Saviour who delivers us from sin and death, and promises eternal life (cf. Psalm 23).[15]

Similarly, other elements of Greek and Roman mythology were given new Christian content and integrated into Graeco-Roman Christology to meet new religious needs in a rapidly expanding world. Another example is the Greek god Orpheus who, with lyre in hand and surrounded by animals, is reinterpreted to represent Christ. Just as Orpheus charmed wild animals so Christ tamed stubborn sinners. Similarly, the story of Orpheus' descent into hell to find his lost wife, Eurydice, was analogous with Christ's harrowing of hell, and was used to help non-Christians to understand the complexities of the resurrection. In using the visible imagery of the catacombs to convey the invisible spiritual content of the faith, early Christians began to develop an artistic language which for Orthodox believers expressed the same truth as the sacred word.[16]

In his masterly work on Jesus through the centuries, Jaroslav Pelikan shows how, with the growth of Christendom, the inculturation of the gospel found expression in ever-changing depictions of Jesus. Accordingly, in each age, 'the life and teachings of Jesus represented an answer (or, more often, *the* answer) to the most fundamental questions of human existence and of human destiny, and it was to the figure of Jesus as set forth in the

Gospels that those questions were addressed'.[17] Furthermore, because each epoch posed different questions, the different portrayals of Jesus provide a key to 'the genius of that age'.[18] Thus, the many faces of Jesus over the centuries reflect both an artistic response to the philosophical and theological quest of the time, and the impact of the gospel story on the cultural, political, social and economic history of each nation.

Pelikan uses a series of 'images of Christ' to chart Jesus' place in the history of European culture. So, for example, he becomes the Rabbi in first-century Judaism, the Light of the World in the Graeco-Roman context, the King of Kings in the Roman Empire, and so on to the Historical Jesus in the eighteenth-century Age of Enlightenment, and the Poet of the Spirit in the art and literature of nineteenth-century Romanticism. As the indigenous response to Christianity became a powerful force in Asia, Latin America and Africa during the nineteenth and twentieth centuries, this had some impact on Europe. New faces of Jesus reflected his prophetic stand against socio-economic and political injustice, and he became identified as Jesus the Champion of Justice for the Poor, the Healer of the Nations, the Liberator, and the Revolutionary.[19] (See Exercise 8 pages 38-39 for a complete list of titles.)

Modern European images of Christ well illustrate the ongoing process of inculturation except that, in stark contrast to earlier European history, the context is now unremittingly secular. In England,

Stanley Spencer (1891-1959) made a radical move in setting the gospel story in the cosy parochialism of his Thameside village of Cookham in Berkshire, 'a holy suburb of heaven', exemplifying the fact that in every age the Christian faith must continue interacting with vernacular culture if it is to survive.[20]

The Bible was central to Spencer's Victorian upbringing and, for him, it came alive in Cookham. The life of Christ takes on new meaning when depicted in ordinary, everyday experiences as in *The Nativity*, re-enacted in a Cookham garden (1912), *The Baptism of Christ* set in the local swimming pool (1952), *The Last Supper* crammed into the confines of a nearby malthouse used for drying hops (c. 1919), and *The Raising of Jairus's Daughter*, with a hysterical family group crowding the bedroom of a modern red-brick house (1947). In a large unfinished painting of the Cookham Regatta, Christ preaches to festive punters from a boat on the banks of the river, while diners disport themselves on the hotel lawn (1957).

Spencer had a profound sense of wonder and of the sacredness of the whole of life. He thought that because Christ had chosen to enter our humanity, it gave human life great dignity, investing everything with holiness. As he explained: 'The instinct of Moses to take his shoes off, when he saw the burning bush, was similar to my feelings. I saw many burning bushes in Cookham. I observed this sacred quality in the most unexpected places.'[21] The way in which his own domestic activities were permeated with spirituality is well illustrated in *The Centurion's Servant* where the centurion (a young Spencer) is sprawled across the maid's bed while he and his brothers kneel alongside in prayer (1914). Again, in *The Marriage at Cana*, Spencer and his first wife Hilda ready themselves amidst the hustle of wedding preparations (1953), while *The Betrayal* takes place in the back garden of his home, with a young Spencer watching the drama unfold from the safety of the school-house next door (1922-23).

Spencer's gift was to confront us with the drama of the gospel story in first-century Jerusalem, while making it readily accessible to all by incarnating Christ in a familiar English setting. In *Christ Carrying the Cross* (1920), our Lord passes the artist's home in Cookham High Street followed by handymen balancing ladders on their shoulders, each absorbed in their own ordained task. Onlookers hang gawping out the windows and all are stolidly indifferent except for Mary, who stands weeping. It is the very ordinariness of this picture which is arresting.

In *The Crucifixion* (1958), Spencer's earlier painting of a scarecrow strung on an iron pole in an abandoned plot (1934), becomes the prototype for the broken body of Christ. The High Street is once more the setting, only now it resembles a wasteland following excavations for new drains. Handymen ferociously hammer in nails on the makeshift cross, while the locals crowd their windows. Spencer's realism reflects his conviction that 'it is we who are "still nailing Christ to the Cross" '.[22]

In his masterly painting of *The Resurrection, Cookham* (1924-27), the bodies of family and friends arise from graves in Cookham churchyard while Spencer and his wife, Hilda, adopt various guises. A feminine Christ holds children in the flower-decked porch, with a much larger God-figure close behind. In the background a pleasure steamer on the River Thames is packed with the resurrected dead, united with their loved ones and on their way to heaven. By connecting the ordinary things of life with the imaginary, Spencer was able to show how everything has a double meaning.

For Spencer, light was 'the holy presence, the substance of God'.[23] This numinous quality is reflected in the series of eight works depicting *Christ in the Wilderness* (1939-55), mirroring Spencer's own wilderness experience when he began the series. His Jewish Christ is modelled on Middle Eastern European refugees in London at the time. Plants and animals of the Berkshire countryside, including meadow flowers, hen and chickens, a fox and a deer, evoke both the artist's belief in the goodness of God's creation and Christ's empathy with nature. In seeking to contextualize the gospel story in his own experience, Spencer exemplifies the ongoing dialogue which is at the heart of inculturation. No wonder that his pictures still resonate with people today.

Mark Cazalet and Dinah Roe Kendall are contemporary British artists who too incarnate Christ in everyday life. However, while Cazalet's dramatic theatrical paintings blend the figurative with the symbolic and the imaginary, Kendall sets her brightly coloured depictions of the gospel narratives in homely situations. In her portrayal of the life of Christ from annunciation to ascension, her family and neighbours become the actors in this dramatically visual retelling of the *The Greatest Story Ever Told*. At the same time, the raw immediacy of her interpretation of well-known gospel events breathes new life into them.[24] The Scottish sculptor, Peter Ball, is equally innovative in transforming detritus and driftwood collected on beaches into sculptures of the Madonna and Christ.[25]

In recent times The Stations of the Cross have inspired a wide range of interpretations in every imaginable medium; for example, Norman Adams' challenging paintings in St Mary's, Mulberry Street, a Roman Catholic church in Manchester, and the sets of Stations that were commissioned to celebrate the millennium in the Eastern Counties.[26] In all these many ways, contemporary British artists continue to wrestle with the question: 'Who is Christ for us today?'

The received Christ versus the indigenous Christ

As the missionary movement gathered momentum in the eighteenth and nineteenth centuries, the image of Jesus exported around the world was invariably Caucasian, and remained firmly so, no matter the culture of those on the receiving end. Testimony, indeed, to an almost universal missionary zeal to convert 'the heathen' to a European form of

Christianity which was inseparably linked with western civilization, and the racism that accompanied it.

An imperial Christianity was matched by an imperial Christ. Moreover, missionary theology put an insidious gloss on the kingly image, making it synonymous with dominance and triumphalism, whereas the original concept of Christ the King saw him as the liberator from all worldly tyrannies. Christ was turned into the patron saint of conquistadores and colonizers, legitimizing conquest and perpetuating subjugation. Such imagery, together with the gentle Jesus of Victorian piety, demanded resignation and submission in the face of oppression, and condemned rebelliousness and insubordination. Converts to Christianity had no choice but to accept an other-worldly Jesus who had little relevance to their lives, and who was used to justify racial prejudice, segregation and exploitation.

Missionary images of Christ remained deeply entrenched in the receptor cultures long after the colonizers had left, bequeathing a dualistic theology which separated the material from the spiritual, the body from the soul. God was kept firmly out of politics and economics, yet, as in South Africa and the United States, was invoked by those in power to support the status quo. It was a religion concerned only with personal salvation, an interior moralistic faith divorced from the totality of people's experience.

However, it was not until the 1960s that Black Power began to make a significant impact in the United States and black prophetic voices became more strident in denouncing the religious and cultural indoctrination endured for centuries. Vincent Harding was one who rejected 'the American Christ':

> This Christ shamed us by his pigmentation, so obviously not our own. He condemned us for our blackness, for our flat noses, for our kinky hair, for our strange power of expressing emotion in singing and shouting and dancing. He was so sedate, so genteel, so white. And as soon as we were able, many of us tried to be like him.[27]

Black Power gave young people the confidence to affirm their blackness and to search for a religious reality that was more faithful to their own experience. The American Methodist Episcopal Church had, in fact, accepted black images of Jesus a hundred years previously, with Bishop Henry Turner declaring that 'God is Negro', convinced that the Jesus of history was a man of colour, an Afro-Asiatic Jew. Nonetheless, in 1970, when Howard University School of Divinity was presented with a picture of a black Christ by its graduating class, they refused to display it. Although this was at the height of black consciousness, and Afro hairstyles and dashikis were fashionable, Africanization had yet to be internalized. Since then the school has become one of the centres of black scholarship.[28]

Among the First Nations or Native American people in North America, the Sioux medicine man, Lame Deer, was equally vociferous in railing against the syncretic-synthetic Jesus of European Christianity:

> You have made a blondie out of Jesus. I don't care for those blonde, blue-eyed pictures of a sanitized, Cloroxed, Ajaxed Christ. How would you like it if I put braids on Jesus and stuck a feather in his hair? You would call me a very crazy Indian, wouldn't you? Jesus was a Jew. He wasn't a yellow-haired Anglo. I am sure he had black hair and a dark skin like an Indian. The white ranchers here wouldn't have let him step out with their daughters and wouldn't have liked him having a drink in their saloons. His religion came out of the desert in which he lived, out of his kind of mountains, his kind of animals, his kind of plants. You've tried to make him into an Anglo-Saxon Fuller Brush salesman, a long-haired Billy Graham in a fancy nightshirt, and that is why he doesn't work for you any more.[29]

Lame Deer is not just protesting about some harmless European image of Christ, or even about a difference in cultural perspective. Like the African-American theologians he is concerned about the socially and politically repressive components of the received tradition:

> The trouble is not with Christianity, with religion, but with what you have made out of it. You have turned it upside down. You have made the religion of the protest leader and

hippie Jesus into the religion of the missionaries, army padres, Bureau of Indian Affairs officials. These are altogether different religions, my friends.[30]

However, these radical insights were slow to make a wider impact. In Southern Africa, loyalty to the received missionary tradition meant unswerving resistance to change until quite recently. No matter that European works of art in churches throughout the land perpetuate a colonized consciousness, or that pictures of a white Jesus with a black satanic figure, which grace many urban black homes, may continue to oppress. Many African people still cling to the belief that the Christian God and his Son are inescapably white. Artistically this has had serious repercussions.

There were the beginnings of change in the mid-1920s when black Anglican students in the Transvaal began to incorporate African motifs in their woodcarvings. But even as the sculptors began to draw more deeply on their indigenous spirituality, European tastes prevailed with religious artefacts being imported from overseas at great expense. Black people, too, put up strong resistance. Dina Cormick recalls the horrified response of Catholic parishioners at Inqwavuma, Zululand, to a Dutch carving of a black Madonna and Christ given to their church in the 1950s. It was soon removed. Later, when two Zulu sculptors began to depict the Holy Family as African, they fared no better. Their compatriots complained that the carvings were either too ugly or too realistic, while others thought that a black image of Christ diminished his status.[31]

Such negativity remains to this day, black clergy included. Fortunately there are those, like Dr Kakhetla in Maseru, who are forthright in saying: 'I don't want a namby-pamby willowy white Jesus, reclining on his disciples' breast; but a Jesus who is one of us, in our situation, where we are. *This* is the Incarnation.'[32]

It was only in the closing decades of the twentieth century that the black conscious-ness movement gained momentum across the globe and that significant numbers of indigenous people began a sustained protest against an oppressive missionary legacy. Third World people consciously started to take responsibility for their own liberation, to become the subjects of their own history, and to read the Scriptures for themselves with new eyes. What they found were fresh images of Jesus who took flesh in their context, their culture and their historical experience. The impact of this is well expressed in a ground-breaking document, *The Road to Damascus*, signed by Christians from seven different nations, with 500 signatories from South Africa alone:

> What we discovered was that Jesus was one of us. He was born in poverty. He did not become incarnate as a king or a nobleman but as one of the poor and oppressed. He took sides with the poor, supported their cause and blessed them. On the other hand, he condemned the rich (Luke 6.20, 24) ... He even described his mission as the liberation of the downtrodden (Luke 4.18). That was the very opposite of what we had been taught. At the heart of Jesus' message was the coming of the Reign of God. We discovered that Jesus had promised the Reign of God to the poor.[33]

As Third World Christians found their voice in expressing radical new christological insights, Liberation Theology in Latin America was followed by as many contextual theologies as there were countries of origin. This indigenous theological impulse was matched by imaginative new portrayals of Jesus in every possible medium. We find images of a black, yellow or brown Christ clothed in the garb of a hundred different nations jockeying alongside depictions of him as the Liberator and the Laughing Christ in Latin America; the Freedom Fighter and the Angry Christ in the Philippines; the Smiling Christ in Korea; the Tattooed Christ in Samoa; the Black Messiah in Southern Africa; the Rasta Jesus (Jesus as Dread) in the Caribbean and the United Kingdom; Christ the Workman in Hong Kong; the Refugee in Uganda and Egypt, or the Dancing Christ in Java.

That is not to say that the missionary legacy has not persisted, sometimes in new guises, such as Christ the Miracle Worker and Magician beloved of rice Christians and followers of the right-wing prosperity gospel, or Jesus the Eschatological Hero. These images foster a privatized spirituality which finds fulfilment in future blessings in the world to come while upholding the status quo in church and society, however oppressive that might be.

The new indigenous Christologies have produced a style and form of art which is as revolutionary as their theological content. At the same time, they remain rooted in the imagery and symbolism of their unique cultural traditions. This worldwide kaleidoscope of images is exemplified in the garish clothing of the Calypso Christ from Jamaica, a Taiwanese crucifixion combining sculpture and laser art, Christ the Enlightened One reflected in Buddhist iconography, the Australian Road to Calvary rendered in the stippled artwork of the aboriginal tradition, a paper cut Chinese nativity, or the resurrected Christ painted in Orthodox Oriental style on an Ethiopian ostrich egg.

The initial impact of these many faces of Christ can be quite shocking to anyone for whom the 'white Christ' is the norm. Western theologians, too, are quick to warn about the dangers of 'syncretism'. They choose to ignore the fact that contextualization has been taking place in Europe during the past 2,000 years, and that discernment has always been necessary to sift the good from the bad in the inculturation process. This is not a modern theological phenomenon, nor is it culture specific.

Because the images come from different cultures, they can also be used in inter-faith studies. Where Christianity is a minority religion, as in the East, the characteristics of other faiths, deeply embedded in the indigenous culture, will inevitably permeate portrayals of Christ. Indirectly, therefore, the images can sensitize us to the spirituality of other faiths, offering an invaluable opportunity for us to see Christ from fresh perspectives. We are thus able to strip our inherited Christology of its diehard Anglo-Saxon underpinnings and rediscover the Middle-Eastern Jewish Jesus of the Bible.

❋ ❋ ❋ ❋ ❋

Exercises with the many faces of Christ

8. Learning about Christ through the centuries

The following list is largely taken from Jaroslav Pelikan, *Jesus Through the Centuries. His Place in the History of Culture.*[34]

- Find images that match the titles for Jesus over the ages. Identify and discuss the differences.

- Images from different eras could provide a framework for teaching Church history and illustrating religious and social change:

The Rabbi – Jesus as teacher and prophet, first-century Judaism.

The Light of the Gentiles – to the Graeco-Roman world, second and third centuries.

The King of Kings – Jesus depicted as all-powerful: lordship of Caesar versus lordship of Christ, Roman Empire, second and third centuries. Constantine's role as both Caesar and a Christian leading to the rise of the 'Christian Empire', fourth century.

The Cosmic Christ – Christ the Logos as the mind, reason and word of God, and meaning of the universe, in Christianized Platonic philosophy, third and fourth centuries.

The Son of Man – Christian anthropology of St Augustine, fifth century.

The True Image – Byzantine icons of the eighth and ninth centuries.

Christ crucified: the saving power of the cross – as against the demonic power of evil in tenth- and eleventh-century literature and art of the Middle Ages.

The Monk or the Ascetic who rules the world – interaction of monasticism and politics in the medieval world. Benedictine understanding of Christ denying the world in order to conquer it, eleventh and twelfth centuries.

The Bridegroom of the Soul – neo-Platonic mysticism in the medieval world.

The Divine and Human Jesus: the Man of Sorrows – St Francis of Assisi's rediscovery of the full humanity of Christ, suffering like us, thirteenth and fourteenth centuries.

Imitation of Christ – Jesus as suffering friend with whom one has long conversations, fifteenth century.

The Universal Man – relating Christ to the humanism of the Renaissance era, fifteenth and sixteenth centuries.

The Mirror of the Eternal – as the Mirror of the True in the new vernacular; as the Mirror of the Beautiful in Reformation art and in the literature of the Catholic Reformation in Spain; as the Mirror of the Good in the Christian politics of Calvin and the Reformed tradition.

The Prince of Peace – 'just wars' and crusades as 'holy war' sanctified in the name of Jesus during the Reformation and Wars of Religion in Europe, together with the resurgence of Christian pacifism.

The Teacher of common sense – going beyond the Christ of dogma to discover a rational system of morals in the Age of Enlightenment, eighteenth century.

The Poet of the Spirit – sweet and sentimental face of Jesus, floating painlessly through life doing good, in the art and literature of nineteenth-century Romanticism.

The historical Jesus – a more human Jesus deeply involved in the issues and struggles of his time, twentieth century.

The Champion of justice for the poor; Jesus the Liberator; Jesus the Revolutionary.

The Man who belongs to the world – Jesus as a world figure, nineteenth and twentieth centuries.

The Jesus of peace, justice and love – the basic challenges of Jesus' message as in films such as *Jesus of Montreal,* twentieth and twenty-first centuries.

9.   Learning from the World Church

Even with a modest collection of pictures a set can be made around a particular theme for teaching, discussion and meditation. The focus may be cultural – Filipino, Australian, British, African or Indian images, or historical – images relating to the Coptic or Celtic periods. It may feature the work of one artist – Alfred Thomas, Frank Wesley and Jyoti Sahi in India (middle to late twentieth century); Bernard Gcwensa, Ruben Xulu and Frans Claerhout in South Africa (middle to late twentieth century); Sadao Watanabe in Japan (mid-twentieth century).

The collected works of different cultural groups offer other insights – Chinese and Indian artists (1940s); African artists in Cyrene, Zimbabwe (twentieth century); the people of Solentiname in Nicaragua (1970s); Asian Christian artists (1970s to the present day). If a biblical theme is being followed, focus on a liturgical season such as Advent, Christmas, Epiphany, Lent, Passion Week (with Stations of the Cross), Easter, Ascensiontide or Pentecost.

9.1 Learning from other contexts and cultures

This exercise offers a way of:

* learning about the worldwide Church;
* identifying with people in other cultures;
* being spiritually enriched by other experiences of the living Christ.

- Images of Christ from different cultures and contexts are set out on display.

- Choose an image from an unfamiliar culture or situation. Meditate on it.

- The group then comes together in a circle with the pictures being placed on the floor for greater visibility.

- Go round the circle asking people what influenced their choice of picture. Are any of the images problematical? If so, discuss.

- Identify artistic and cultural differences. What does this tell us about Christ incarnated in different contexts and cultures?

- What aspect of Christ has been emphasized? Why do you think this is so?

E.g. the Dancing Christ in Asia, the Indian Christ sitting in a lotus position; Christ as Healer and Teacher in Africa, the suffering Christ in Latin America, Christ with the poor and oppressed, Christ as a refugee, Christ with children in China and Japan, etc.

- What can we learn from the images about other cultures and contexts?

- How easy is it to receive a new understanding of Jesus?

9.2 Titles for Christ in other cultures

In different cultures and contexts Jesus has been depicted as:

Teacher, Healer, Prophet, Guru, Holy Man, Enlightened Being, Shaman, Miracle Worker, Magician, Story Teller, Liberator, Freedom Fighter, Political Martyr, Refugee, Suffering Christ, Angry Christ, Black Messiah, Dread Christ (England and Caribbean), Calypso Christ, Christ Present in the Poor, Inner-City Christ, God's Fool, The Good Shepherd (with variations for herders of different animals), Christ the Mother, Gentle Jesus, Hollywood Hero, Eschatological Hero, Christus Victor, Worker Christ, Dancing Christ (Asia), Holy Child (Philippines and Spain), Dalit Christ (India), The Colonial Christ (of oppression), The Unknown Christ of Hinduism, The Unbound Christ, etc.

- Titles of Christ can be used as a framework for teaching about different aspects of Third World theology.

- Find images to match some of the titles. What new understanding does this give us about Christ as incarnated in these cultures?

- Give your own titles to selected images and then compare these with those given by the artists. Discuss the differences.

- Images with the same subject can be compared in different cultures, in order to gain new insight into well-worn themes, e.g. the Good Shepherd, Christ with children, Christ as healer and teacher, Worker Christ, the Suffering Christ, Christ the Liberator.

9.3 The parables of Christ

The parables of Christ as depicted in different cultures can give us a new understanding of Christ's teaching, more especially the Good Samaritan, the Prodigal Son and the Wise and Foolish Virgins.

9.4 The Christ we share in other cultures

'Who do you say I am?'

Even as Jesus' disciples responded to this question with different answers, so have there been a variety of responses in different cultures and different situations. Third World images of

Christ help us to reflect theologically on how the gospel has been inculturated in diverse contexts.

9.4.1 *The Christ We Share* resource pack

- This pack has been produced by the United Society for the Propagation of the Gospel (USPG), Church Mission Society (CMS) and the Methodist Church in Britain. It provides a wealth of ideas for activities and worship using 32 images of Christ from different parts of the world, 12 of these being duplicated on acetate for overhead projection.

- The purpose of the pack is to enable a group to engage with a variety of Third World theological perspectives and to examine issues which might arise in the process. Information is given about both the images and Third World theology. The activities have both a global and a local dimension, encouraging participants to discover what their learning about different world theologies might mean for their own communities.

- Sheets are enclosed with ideas for prayer and worship.

- The pack is designed for local churches, schools and colleges.

9.4.2 Identifying different cultures

- Provide a numbered selection of images from different cultures. Working in pairs, ask people to try to identify where they come from. In a brief plenary session compare the answers.

- Discussion can focus on similarities and differences between cultures as depicted in the images, e.g.
  * In a post-colonial context the emphasis might be on cultural representations of Christ – the African or Asian Christ.
  * In a situation of oppression as in the Philippines or Latin America, the focus might be on the Suffering Christ or Christ the Liberator.
  * Can we talk about the Suffering Christ in Britain? What might he look like?

- Discuss any difficulties participants might have with representations of Christ in different cultures. These might be aesthetic, cultural, artistic or theological.

9.4.3 *Born Among Us* resource pack

This pack explores images of the nativity of Christ from around the world. Included in the pack are 16 colour images on acetate and card, all-age worship materials, a nativity play, carol service and eight regional activity sheets. The purpose of the resource is to:
  * discover the relevance of Jesus born among us today;

* explore the birth of Jesus through the eyes of Christian artists around the world;
* learn about Christmas in different cultures;
* worship at Christmas inspired by the vision of the World Church.

9.4.4 Using Third World images of Christ for teaching

* Different themes can be selected for teaching about Third World theology e.g.:
  * African, Asian or Native American faces of Christ;
  * Christ the Liberator in South Africa, Korea, Latin America or the Philippines;
  * Christ the Holy One and Teacher in different Asian countries;
  * The Suffering Christ in the context of the HIV/AIDS pandemic;
  * Christ the Mother: what does this mean in different cultures?
  * Christ the Refugee in Africa or Christ in the Wilderness.

* Compare Third World images with contemporary western ones.

9.5 Working with crosses and crucifixes

I also do workshops with my collection of about 350 crosses and crucifixes from around the world. This can be replicated by inviting people to bring their own crosses and crucifixes and getting them to share:

* something of the story behind them – when, where and how they acquired them.

* what they have meant to the owners on their journeys of faith.

* The crosses and crucifixes can be set out on a table. People are then invited to choose one, but handle with care. Discussion takes place as with images. Because this resource is both tactile and personal it evokes a completely different response compared to the pictures.

* Ask people to choose between a cross and a crucifix from the pooled selection. Discuss the theological issues involved in their choice.

* In an extended workshop people can enjoy making their own crosses and crucifixes. This can include collages with pictures cut from magazines and newspapers. Suitable resource material must be supplied.

3

Reaching People on the Edge

'Father knows best'

Who are the people on the edge? From the Church's point of view, they include agnostics, people who seek spiritual nourishment from other religious traditions, those who attend church only occasionally or have left altogether, and the so-called 'unreached' for whom religion is an irrelevance. Of greater concern, though, are those within the Church whose faith has never actually been brought to life in a transformative experience. They may well be the mainstay of a church, active in doing good works, fund-raising and the rest; but do they have a living faith? Do they have any sense of vocation? I speak from my own experience of having been a professional lay person, on numerous committees and synods, but basically untouched by the good news of the gospel.

As an Anglican of Catholic persuasion, my faith was shaped by a disciplined sacramental tradition. School at St Cyprian's, on the slopes of Table Mountain in Cape Town, was the closest thing to a nunnery. From early morning, our days were regimented by the ringing of a bell and marked by unquestioning obedience to authority. We attended chapel twice daily, adorned with white veils, and fasted before receiving Holy Communion. On Sundays we attended Matins or Choral Evensong in St George's Cathedral, clothed in shapeless white dresses, black stockings and panama hats.

I learnt chunks of the catechism, the *Book of Common Prayer* and the Bible by heart. I was prepared for confirmation by the Dean of Cape Town, was confirmed by Archbishop Geoffrey Clayton, a former Cambridge don, and heard some of the finest preachers of the day, many fresh off the boat from England. But this undigested regimen of religious instruction bore little relevance to home life on a farm, to the introverted anxieties of an immature schoolgirl, or to the daunting post-war world outside.

Racism was deeply embedded in our upbringing and white minority power and privilege accepted as the norm. The increasingly repressive Afrikaner regime went unquestioned. The enduring symbiosis of Mother Church and British Crown continued to inform our English-speaking lives no matter what political changes there were. Our first South African bishop was not elected until 1952, a century after the Church's founding, and the first African bishop in 1960. The density of our theological diet, the formalized rituals of the Church, and the heavy presence of authority stifled any spontaneous religious response I might have made even if I had realized this was possible.

For sure, this education sowed seeds of social concern. We knitted for poor starving children during Lent while the headmistress read improving stories of courageous missionaries in foreign parts. After a powerful sermon by the saintly Bishop of Ovamboland, I even had a fleeting vision of being a nun. But my perception of mission remained firmly locked in the Victorian tradition of condescending charity.

In retrospect I am grateful that some vestiges of the mystery of faith managed to permeate my adolescent psyche. I think especially of Cranmer's magisterial prose, even if it was incomprehensible at the time. So too, I came to value regular eucharistic worship; glorious cathedral music in the best of British traditions; singing in a not-so-glorious chapel choir; the ordered rhythm of the liturgical year; and, above all, the peace that permeates the fabric of a church blessed by faithful worship. These became the foundations on which I later built a living faith, for although my Christian formation was sound, any sense of a personal relationship with Christ passed me by. Rather, a stern God loomed menacingly, ever ready to pounce on my pathetic misdemeanours. The obligatory twice-yearly confession to the Dean was a dreaded humiliation as I sorrowfully repented of my unremitting boredom with a suffocating diet of religion. The sense of failure to live up to expectations was simply overwhelming, as was my plummeting self-esteem.

As an Anglican, it seemed that I was there to attend services and be head-counted. I was drilled in learning when and where to stand, sit, kneel, genuflect, bow, close my eyes, find the right pages, adopt the right posture, mouth the right responses, and have my collection at the ready – and woe betide me if I got it wrong. For me, worship was defined by right behaviour and military precision. The Church did a thorough job in burdening me with guilt about my supposed unworthiness, and hang-ups about the do's and dont's of life. These can so easily masquerade as the core of Christian belief, reinforcing the power of the clergy and shackling the laity with remorse.

I believe that the Church is there to raise disciples and to mediate faith. But it still spends an inordinate amount of time and energy processing people through the rites of passage – baptism, confirmation, marriage, last rites – on a kind of conveyor belt. A church member is thus reduced to a cypher, a statistical detail in the 'league table' of figures by which the Church assesses its likely survival. Boosting attendance figures by including people at weekday services and special acts of worship may say something about belonging but do they tell us anything about believing? Are most regular churchgoers clear about their faith? Are they confident in expressing and sharing it? Perhaps the reality is too awful to contemplate.

I, for one, left school with a good measure of the Articles of Faith, but no faith to live by. Faith is a life-giving gift which I eventually received from an unexpected quarter. The wake-up call came 20 years later when I began doctoral studies. My research focused on the religious and social history of the Xhosa-speaking people and involved regular field trips to the former Ciskei and Transkei. How shocked I was to be asked to witness to my faith: to give an account of the Christian hope within me! Consumed with embarrassment, I stumbled and stuttered through a poor apology for being a Christian.

Working alongside heroic African people during the spiralling horror of the apartheid years changed my life. It was enormously humbling to see how they confronted the daily onslaught of deprivation, violence and oppression with a steadfast faith that some day God's justice would triumph over evil. Through their prophetic witness I came to discover something of what being a disciple of Christ was really about. In the long term, I felt challenged to find ways of seeing how lay people could learn to take responsibility for their own spiritual development, and be motivated and equipped to put their faith into action. This became a lifelong passion and remains so today.

From 1988 until 2001 I worked in various capacities in the Church of England. To my surprise I discovered that my own experience of disempowerment in my religious formation was widespread among Anglican laity and, for many, it was almost overwhelming. I cannot speak for other denominations. As a missioner, my challenge was to get lay people to come clean and address the problem openly and honestly, without fear of censure. Only then were they free to rediscover their faith and grow in confidence in developing and sharing it.

A major difficulty in tackling these issues is the chronic dependency of so many lay people on their clergy, of a learned helplessness. Their subservience to the hierarchical status quo remains deeply entrenched, militating against independent initiatives in both thought and action. It is hard to penetrate years, if not decades, of conditioning which holds fast to the notion that the way to God is through a priest. Among the old guard, the incumbent is often thought to defend the gates of heaven with unrelenting power. This sustains an endemic conservatism of the 'Father knows best' school of churchmanship, an 'Our Father theology' which encourages laity to collude with clergy domination.

Another problem area is the laity's efforts to keep their ignorance about doctrinal matters secret from their clergy. Their fear of being found out is debilitating. This is conspicuous in the power games played out in church gatherings and meetings. Pious platitudes and theological jargon are spewed forth freely to impress, leaving the less articulate mute and impotent. But verbal window-dressing may well conceal serious gaps in Christian understanding, making those who hog the floor vulnerable to being exposed, while the quiet ones, too intimidated to compete, remain without a voice.

The fact that too many clergy have become imprisoned within the precise formulations of systematic theology and doctrinal orthodoxy does not help. It is bad enough that their preaching invariably passes over the heads of 'their flock'. But this obfuscation of theology also reinforces the low esteem of their parishioners as well as failing to address their immediate concerns. Laurie Green, a Church of England bishop, cites graffiti on a theological wall as an example of just how ridiculously intimidating the intellectual approach can be: 'Jesus said to them, "Who do you say that I am?" They replied, "You are the eschatalogical manifestation of the ground of our being, in which kerygma we find the ultimate meaning in our interpersonal relationships". And Jesus replied, "What?" '[1]

Too often, Church teaching has consisted of feeding the laity a diet of stereotypical Christology, which they are then expected to regurgitate in their prayers, confessions and testimonies without owning the theology or experiencing the Christ typified by it. One has immense empathy for those who soldier on against such odds, and perhaps even more for those who have given up the struggle and left the Church disenchanted, if not embittered. This is not to denigrate those faithful clergy who humbly and lovingly feed their flock with a profundity of simple gospel truths and a lifetime's experience of pastoral wisdom, week after week, year after year.

In Britain, the comparatively recent proliferation of user-friendly catechism courses such as Alpha, Emmaus, Christian Basics (CPAS) and This is our Faith (Affirming Catholicism), have helped enormously in giving lay people confidence in articulating their faith. The new emphasis on relating religious questions to real life is affirming of people's experience, no matter who they are or where they come from. But ultimately this remains an intellectual approach, under Church control. The faith is still taught through verbal communication based on reason, argument and logic. The ability to comprehend is still dominated by words.

I believe that every praying Christian is a theologian, and that a person's theology should be relevant to his or her life of faith. Each one of us has the birthright to know God and to be able to witness in one's own unique way. For too long theology has been the jealously guarded preserve of clergy and academics. True mission happens when the people of God are empowered by the Holy Spirit to proclaim the word and to give utterance to their faith with or without words (Joel 2.28-29; Acts 2.4, 17-18). The calling of lay people is to free themselves from the constraints of the institutional Church and do their own theology without priestly mediation or control.

At the same time, working with images has enabled many clergy to rediscover their vocation or even find a new direction in their ministry. Their personal prayer life has been enriched, their preaching revitalized, their insight into where the laity are coming from greatly enhanced. For clergy, it is a challenge to work alongside laity as partners in the journey of faith. They must remain open and vulnerable as they seek the mind of Christ in this new venture.

Touching the hem of the living Christ

Working with images of Christ in England, Wales, Canada and South Africa has proved to be a profound spiritual experience for a whole range of groups, ranging in size from a handful to hundreds. The multiracial, intercultural and ecumenical dimensions have been of particular significance. Above all, the response of lay people has been amazing. Like the woman with the flow of blood (Luke 8.43-48), an extraordinary number do not consider themselves worthy to encounter Christ face to face. Exercises using images of Christ seem to endow them with the courage and confidence to develop their own faith, instead of accepting the received faith of the Church.

This work is rooted in a unique theology of mission which values people for who they are, enabling them to unburden themselves of inherited misconceptions of Church teaching and rediscover, nurture and articulate their faith in their own words. Moreover, the images offer a radical new way of reflecting on faith in relation to contemporary life, encouraging people to be more outward-looking and to grapple with the wider issues of the world. For many people, it is a brave step to do theology both individually and collectively,

as members of a community of faith, without having to walk the tightrope of doctrinaire God-talk. As they use the images they can experience joy and freedom, many for the first time in their lives, as they become enthused with the Spirit of God.

In his 30 years in a Durham parish, the vicar had never before heard members of his Parochial Church Council talk openly about Christ. But with a picture in their hands, they were able to find the words to say what they really believed, honestly and unashamedly. Being confronted with people's testimonies of faith is often a revelation to clergy because they suddenly realize that their parishioners are not where they thought they were in their spiritual journey.

We have found that after a workshop, people who have never publicly talked about Christ before continue to do so for weeks, if not months. People have wanted to talk to me in the most unlikely places – a railway station platform, dress shop, market place, in the street, the cathedral toilet – as they wanted to recall the images they worked with, what these meant to them, and how their lives have been affected. In one evangelical Anglican parish, the incumbent was less than enthusiastic about using images in an evening presentation but pressure from his lay team prevailed. Three weeks later he found to his utter amazement that his parishioners were still talking enthusiastically about Christ, and wanting to know more. Alpha and Emmaus courses followed.

Working with images can hold other surprises. Once, when working with my Diocesan Bishop, we invited a rural deanery group to reflect on their journey of faith by comparing images of who Christ might have been for them as children with who he was for them now. The bishop spoke about how our image of Christ changes and matures as we grow older. He was vociferously challenged by one woman, who maintained that Christ had remained the same for her throughout her life. This is common with images of Christ as loving shepherd and protector of children. In such instances, people might need to be resourced in their faith development so that they can see the possibility of spiritual growth.

A workshop in a theological college also brought unexpected results. In selecting images for who they thought Christ was for their college, five groups of ordinands whittled their pictures down to almost identical images. These showed symbolic representations of a fractured, fragmented Christ with sharp points protruding at every angle. In the ensuing discussion, the ordinands claimed that while the college aimed to project a perfect image to the outside world, their experience was of pain, tension and a lack of trust. Almost without exception they confessed to suppressing their uncertainties and problems for fear of being found wanting and their apprehension that this might be held against them in the assessment of their suitability for ordination. Two women left the room in tears. There was

much that needed to be addressed, and the principal was so advised.

In quite different circumstances, images have been used with a range of church groups to expose sensitive issues which might otherwise not have surfaced. These have included leadership difficulties, the rightful delegation of power and responsibility, unresolved tensions in a team ministry, problems with inter-personal relations, past hurts that have not been addressed, ethical issues, and conflicting views on the direction in which a church or fellowship should move.

All-age workshops have enabled people across three generations to come together to share their faith and to stretch their imaginations. The insights of young people continue to amaze and to challenge. Three girls in one parish group chose *No More Mr Nice Guy* as their image of Christ, a cover illustration of a Student Christian Movement magazine in 1994. A laid-back looking Christ is depicted with orange hair, a green crown of thorns and a glowing cigarette between his lips. The editorial was just as challenging: 'The sugar-coated Jesus has to go. The image of Jesus as universal Mr Nice Guy is as familiar and comforting as a shabby teddy bear and as much use. *No More Mr Nice Guy* invites us to think again about Jesus, to shed our sentimental imagery in favour of a Jesus who has direct relevance to our age, who speaks to our concerns and who *bites*.' While many adults found the picture offensive, the girls felt that such an image would provoke their school-friends to discover more.

In a former pit village, a class of pre-primary schoolchildren worked with images of the nativity and then drew their own pictures. These were compiled into a book with their comments, providing considerable insight into their home situations. Again, during a time of racial tension in a troubled multiracial school in south London, I worked alongside a gifted art teacher with a class of teenagers. Each student chose an image of Christ and then made their own interpretations of the pictures in different media – paint, crayon, charcoal and clay. Some students were from different faith backgrounds, others from none. Most had little or no knowledge of Christianity. The subsequent discussion was an eye-opener as they asked penetrating questions about who this Christ was and why he had been depicted so differently in different cultures. They then reflected on their own artwork and what they themselves had tried to achieve. This is a yet untapped resource for what is commonly known as pre-evangelism.

Baptism preparation is another opportunity for pre-evangelism or for awakening a dormant faith. Sheila Day, Mission Enabler and Reader in Durham Diocese, uses images as a way of drawing out what parents already know or feel about Jesus, helping them to own the discussion. Apart from the prime favourites, the photograph of Robert Powell as Jesus of Nazareth in the television movie (*The Christ We Share*, no. 27) is extremely popular, with Christmas card nativities and plain crosses. Parents are also encouraged to use pictures when talking to older children.

The basic workshops have proved to be a powerful means of unlocking a dormant spiritual potential, suppressed by the structural weight of the Church. Most people have no problem in relating to a picture and surprise even themselves at how easily they begin talking about Christ with minimal self-consciousness. But the exercises can also be an emotive experience, opening people up to deeply repressed feelings. An Anglican ordinand, dragooned into attending a workshop, was amazed when a couple of Latin American images 'spoke' to her with great immediacy. She wept as she began to share the pain of the death of an adopted Nicaraguan girl some years previously. For her it was a cathartic experience to revisit long suppressed issues. At the same time, the way in which even strangers are able to comfort one another is extraordinarily moving.

In Wales, an elderly bard chose *The Tortured Christ*, an image of a skeletal Christ doubled up in agony on the cross. The original was sculpted by the Brazilian artist, Guido Rocha, who had been wrongfully imprisoned and severely tortured in his homeland (*The Christ We Share*, no. 2). He survived the horror of his incarceration by identifying the agony of Christ with the torment suffered by himself and fellow prisoners. Through his sculpture Rocha was able to express his belief that God's grace overcomes all evil. Many people have used this image as a focus for prayer and meditation in identifying with the suffering of oppressed people. The Welsh bard, however, had advanced cancer and he equated the agony of Christ with his own experience of extreme pain. In sharing something of his suffering with colleagues, he found release in a lyrical outpouring of poetry in his native tongue.

The Angry Christ from the Philippines (*The Christ We Share*, no. 9) is another image which unlocks powerful feelings. The original was painted by Lino Pantebon (1975) from the Negros islands and depicts a furious Christ with the long hair and beard of a sugar plantation worker. He points an accusing finger at the local sugar barons, who exploit the workers through starvation wages and oppressive feudal conditions. But it is an image which transcends cultural constraints, finding common cause with a black youth worker in South Africa struggling to reconcile past hurts, a Native American chief confronting the Canadian government over indigenous land rights, a Hartlepool pensioner enraged about punitive council taxes, or an Oxford don incensed about world debt.

In quite another context, the images have been useful as an ice-breaker in large gatherings. I well remember an Open Synod conference at Swanwick in Derbyshire, when 200 delegates braved appalling weather conditions to arrive somewhat traumatized and exhausted in the dark. Working in small groups, the images helped participants to calm down, become focused, and enter into the spirit of the gathering. On another occasion, Durham Deanery Synod was meeting in a freezing cold hall with a storm raging outside. Yet the groups could barely be persuaded to part with their images, so engrossed were they in discussing theology and sharing their faith.

The images have also been used successfully in team-building. In Rochester Diocese, clergy and laity worked together in three separate archdeaconry groups to address the question: 'Who is Christ for our church?' An unexpected finding was that a good number of teams were so frenetically busy carrying out their various ministries that they seldom came together to pray, to reflect on the gospel, to support each other, or to share their vision of mission. Plans were immediately made to rectify the situation. Similar findings have surfaced in working with other such groups.

All-clergy groups have their own dynamic as vulnerability with colleagues can be extremely challenging. A favourite picture is *Christ of St John of the Cross*, painted by Salvador Dali in 1951, with the crucified Christ suspended in mid-air as he looks down on the world. Its familiarity offers safety. Braver souls choose more uncomfortable images such as the woman taken in adultery, Zacchaeus up a tree, Peter walking on water, with the other disciples on stormy seas, or asleep with them in the Garden of Gethsemane. Before the ordination of Anglican women, a deacon chose a North American picture by José Clemente Orozco. It portrays Christ standing in front of a huge pile of discarded weaponry, with raised fist and holding an axe, triumphant in having chopped down the cross. It said much about the woman's feelings at the time.

For some clergy, working with images has inspired renewal in their ministry. A rural dean came to a fresh sense of his priestly vocation through meditating on an image of Peter receiving the keys of the kingdom of heaven (Matthew 16.19); while a picture of Christ in the wilderness opened the way for a parish priest to begin spiritual direction. In different dioceses, one bishop had the courage to focus on doubting Thomas, while another identified with Peter's denial of Christ. All expressed surprise at how the pictures had spoken to them. Using images in clergy training in South Africa has not only exposed interracial and gender issues, but has also been a way of finding healing and reconciliation in a non-threatening environment. Clergy are now using images in confirmation and adult education classes in a wide spectrum of parishes.

Stephen Conway, Archdeacon of Durham, reflects on the day I led for his PCC in 1999, as a way of encapsulating the workshop experience. We went to a neutral venue about 20 miles away. The hope was that working with images would involve the whole group, so breaking some of the traditional clergy dependency and giving a voice to those who rarely participated in regular meetings. He recalls:

> Everyone joined in willingly. The images were varied and I was intrigued to see what people would choose. One person was an artist and she chose striking abstract images. Most PCC members, however, opted for strongly realistic images. Not everyone picked traditional images; but most did. Of course, images of the Cross were chosen, while some were drawn to 'soft' images of Jesus as Shepherd and as the Saviour who suffers the little children to come to him. As each person described his or her response to their chosen images, even the shyest member was unusually eloquent. Those not known for being very reflective in public were able to be perceptive about both their images and their own faith journey.

> The exercise was productive on a number of fronts. It certainly met the objectives which had been agreed beforehand. It further illustrated very clearly for me the importance of the humility required of priests and all those in Christian leadership to empty a space for others to grow into. It demonstrated the value of lay leadership in nurturing the people of God. The Images workshop is also the place where our assumptions of our spirituality can be safely reviewed and then safely challenged. It did not leave any of us in the same place. We all moved on, not only in our relationship to Christ but in our relationships with each other. We already cared for each other; but we learned that we could still surprise one another and deepen our respect for each other. Council meetings were never the same again!

However, many clergy find it difficult to relinquish enough authority to give people the freedom to grapple with issues of faith and doctrine. I have frequently been urged to 'tell it like it is', to make some orthodox credal statement as a corrective to any possible heresies that might be expressed. But the theological niceties, as defined by clergy of different traditions, can be hugely disparate. Rather than risk being censured and scorned by their incumbent, many church members have 'gone underground' with what might be considered an unorthodox, home-grown theology.

Working with images can provide a good foundation for catechetical teaching and spiritual training, but careful listening to people's questions must come first. Their concerns, doubts, anxieties and fears all surface in workshops. Following workshop experiences, some people have been inspired to make their own collection of images which they use in house groups, baptism and confirmation classes, youth work, Bible study, meditation and prayer cells, and church displays. Giving people space to do theology for themselves, rooted in their own experience, is at the heart of our God-given mission. This is what makes this mission theology both contextual and incarnational.

The village of Whalton, Northumberland, celebrated the millennium by giving each resident a disposable camera to record their favourite local images. A local artist, Ian Johnson of Broomhill, then cut out small sections of the photographs to produce a montage of the face of Christ, 6ft by 4ft 6in, which is now displayed in the twelfth-century parish church of St Mary Magdalene. The collage consists of 2,850 individual pieces and includes stone walls, gates, gardens, trees, fields, red post-boxes, road signs, animals and birds of every description, bicycles, cars, tractors, children, couples, pensioners, a young hunter with a dead fox, parts of the church, houses, in fact everything that makes up the community and the natural world in which it is set. It is a classic example of how the Holy Spirit has inspired a lay Christian to see the face of Christ in and through and among the people of God and God's creation. In this way the incarnate God becomes a reality in our lives, a visible image of the Body of Christ accessible to all people and all ages (see cover picture).

Mission on the home front

Working as Area Secretary for a British Mission Society was a sobering experience. 'Mission' had suffered a bad press and parishioners advised me to avoid using the word. It has become inextricably linked with the past missionary endorsement of imperialism and colonialism, and the legacy of guilt that resulted from it. From a secular point of view 'mission' has been stripped of any religious meaning and co-opted into business parlance. 'Mission statements' have become the stuff of strategic planning in the workaday world. No church body would have had the courage to emblazon the words 'We're on a Mission' on their vehicles as did the Morrisons chain stores in north-east England. (Their mission is 'to bring you the very best value, week in, week out'.)

My brief was to raise funds from supporting churches and to educate them about mission. This was generally understood as involving one-way traffic from the richer West to the suffering poor in some distant land. Such ideas were reinforced by tear-jerking pictures of famine-starved babies clawing at their mothers' flaccid breasts, or snapshots of exotically dressed indigenous people struggling to survive in drought-stricken or war-torn terrain. There was precious little sense that overseas mission was a reciprocal process: that we could learn and receive much from our mission partners worldwide in addition to any charitable giving. At the same time, it was a struggle to convince parishes that mission was primarily about living the gospel here and now in our own backyard. The fact that I was later appointed Adviser in *Local* Mission in Durham Diocese was a huge help in raising awareness. But what do we mean by 'mission'?

In his magisterial work, *Transforming Mission*, David J. Bosch surveys the entire sweep of Christian history and finds that in the latter half of the twentieth century most denominations subscribed to a theology of mission as *missio Dei*. Accordingly, mission is always God's mission, not ours, to the world. God is a God-for-people and the Church exists because there is mission, not vice versa. Mission is, therefore, 'the good news of God's love, incarnated in the witness of the community, for the sake of the world'.[2] We are challenged to become co-missioners with God. By careful listening, we can try to discern what God is already doing in the world and see how we can be involved. Moreover, as we express our faith in the liberating mission of Jesus, we need to ensure that our proclamation of the gospel through words and witness is matched by our living out the gospel in every facet of our daily lives. This calls for compassion and a sacrificial love which actively seeks to bring about justice and peace, and has a concern for the whole of creation.

In the mid 1990s, Robert Warren's work on building missionary congregations provided the incentive for British churches to move from maintenance to mission, or from 'inherited mode' to 'emerging mode'. Warren's timely contribution was to develop ideas pioneered by the World Council of Churches and present them as an urgent challenge to the Church. He defines a missionary congregation as 'a church which takes its identity, priorities, and agenda, from participation in God's mission in the world ... a church whose presence is incarnate in the surrounding culture'.[3]

However, it is not an easy task to get churches to move out from their well-worn ruts and begin thinking about change. This is especially so if they are struggling to survive. Their energy is taken up with maintaining buildings and scraping together enough funds to meet expenses. So how does one change the mind-set of good faithful people locked into outdated modes of thinking and motivate them into positive action?

I believe that our mission programmes must be unapologetically Christ-centred from the start. Any priorities, any strategies, any plans of action are bound to fail unless we have a living relationship with Christ. Too often, we start our programmes in the wrong place. We assume that just because people attend church regularly and are actively involved, that they are also mission-oriented. Bitter disappointment follows when, after an enthusiastic start, our cherished plans peter out. Unless Christ is at the centre of our being, thinking and doing, we might as well save our energy, our time and our money for church bazaars and other fund-raising activities that help simply to keep the church open.

This is where exercises with images of Christ are invaluable in getting mission onto the church agenda. They help people to understand the meaning of mission, and also offer a way forward into action. If cultural, social, racial or ecumenical elements are included in the exercises they will help people come together to explore gospel challenges in a shared context.

I have used the exercises in Wales, with ecumenical groups of Welsh- and English-speaking clergy from different denominations (including Welsh bards); with Native American and non-Native clergy in Canada, with a racial mix of ministers in South Africa, and with African people from different tribal backgrounds. In England, the diversity of groupings has included a cross-section of social classes, different mixes of culture and race, different denominations, and a wide range of inner-city, suburban and rural representations. The mission exercises have also been used with every conceivable church fellowship including PCCs, cell groups, parish away-days, ordination training, clergy chapters, women's groups, industrial mission and student chaplaincies, and shared ministry teams. Without exception, the images have provided an imaginative new way of focusing on mission.

This method requires participants to move from a quiet inner reflection on personal spirituality, as in the Basic Exercise, to thinking about a corporate spirituality which looks outward in mission. They are also encouraged to actively defend their faith in order to gain greater confidence in expressing their beliefs in a supportive environment. It is an excellent starter for evangelism while the fun element is integral to the experience.

The group is divided into clusters of three or four who remain together throughout the session. The images are displayed on tables as before and every participant is asked to select a picture which for them encapsulates the mission intention of their particular faith community. At this stage we focus on what might be the ideal situation. The question is:

How would our image of Christ serve as a *visual mission statement* for our church or fellowship?

As a *visual mission statement*, the chosen image needs to be readily under-stood by non-participants, especially those with little or no knowledge of Christianity, without any explanation. The objective is to communicate God's love and concern for people through non-verbal imagery that is as relevant to those outside the Church as to those within. Typical pictures of mission include Jesus with groups of people from all over the world – healing, teaching, feeding, celebrating and challenging; Christ as Liberator, Suffering Servant and Good Shepherd; Christ on the cross; symbolic aspects of the Eucharist; and people's involvement together as a community.

After selecting a picture, participants return to their seats and meditate in silence until all are ready and have had time for reflection. Working together as a group, they then take turns to explain why they have chosen a particular image. Passion is a crucial element in this process as people move from faith-sharing to apologetics, from empathetic listening to a vigorously reasoned defence of the good news as embodied in an image of Christ.

Whereas most people struggle to define mission, imagery provides an easy way of opening up the discussion. Each group is then asked to agree on just one image to summarize the mind of their group. Animated debate invariably follows as cluster members strenuously defend their chosen pictures as they attempt to whittle them down to a single image. The dynamics of decision-making and people's coping mechanisms as their pictures are rejected can be very revealing. Humour can provide a happy release. It is significant, too, to see how shy members find their voice as they get caught up in the excitement of the exercise. As the discussion continues the group may have problems in agreeing on one image and

choose to describe a composite picture that embraces their different perceptions.

The session ends with a spokesperson from each group reporting back to the whole group. In turn, a brief report is given on what informed their decision-making process. The reasons given for discarding certain images not only reveal a progression in their mission thinking, but, even more importantly, how unself-consciously they began to do theology together.

Time permitting, the groups can vie with each other in getting their respective image chosen as *the* visual mission statement for the fellowship. Again, the mere fact of having to defend an image refines one's missiological thinking. One parish from Gateshead took 70 of their members, ranging in age from school-children to mid-eighties, on a mission weekend. Passions reached fever pitch as successive group competed against each other to have their picture singled out to represent the mission of their parish. Some participants even climbed on tables better to plead their group's case. Anything that inspires such enthusiasm for mission must be welcomed.

This exercise can provide a faith-based group with a shared motivation for change, the more so as it is Christologically based. As before, the selected images can be used as a focus for prayer, meditation and worship, giving members a chance to offer up their hopes and fears to God. The second stage of the exercise involves analysis, theological reflection, and planning for action.

Action stations with images

In order to retain the momentum of the first stage of the mission exercise, planning for action should follow as soon as possible. Once more, images can be used in the pastoral (hermeneutical) cycle, popularly known as the *See, Judge, Act* model.[4] But first, the fellowship must decide on the issue to be tackled. Working through the *Growing Healthy Churches* material, devised by Robert Warren and myself, would be one way of identifying pressing issues.[5] The range of possibilities is somewhat daunting and could include prayer and spirituality, worship, leadership, relationships within the faith community, growth in discipleship, facing the cost of change, ecumenical involvement, justice and peace issues, partnership with the World Church, working alongside the local community in areas such as homelessness, HIV/AIDS, or in provision for older people, the disadvantaged or children.

An example of an all-encompassing issue would be: 'How to develop the life and mission of our faith community'. We begin the pastoral cycle with *See*, with a group's own experience setting the scene. An analysis of the present situation in the church or fellowship is initiated by asking each participant to choose a picture in response to the question:

Which image of Christ best reflects the present life and mission of our faith community?

Using the now familiar basic exercise, participants first meditate on their chosen image, then share in small groups, followed by feedback to a plenary session. Images of Christ are simply a means to bring the faith community's story to life. The selected images may well be painfully honest in portraying an exclusive, inward-looking fellowship, more concerned with what takes place within its confines than without. Working with images seems to penetrate even the most indomitable defences to expose the reality, however uncomfortable that might be.

An analysis of the faith community's life and mission can be sharpened by working through such issues as:

- the good things, and the not so good things, about the faith community;

- those things that need to be affirmed and developed;

- those things that do not work and need to be discarded;

- what is missing and needs to be introduced.

An analysis of the context in which the faith community finds itself is also necessary so that an outward-looking focus in mission will relate to the needs of the local community, whether these are material, cultural, spiritual, pastoral or physical. There is an abundance of published material relating to church mission audits and needs assessment surveys if a more detailed analysis is required.[6]

Moving on in the cycle to *Judge*, time is now given to prayer and theological reflection. In his book, *Let's Do Theology,*

Laurie Green has an excellent chapter on 'Reflection', which gives advice on choosing appropriate biblical themes and passages, together with a range of imaginative approaches in allowing the Bible to speak to people's experience.[7] Images of Christ are another 'way in', through meditation, Bible study or bibliodrama. A spread of images helps to stimulate the imagination, but even one or two will suffice.

The discussion which follows flows naturally into the last part of the cycle – *Act*. Issues that have surfaced during the *Judge* stage will require a considered response, leading to praxis – action based on theological reflection. Bible study is a common pursuit in British churches, but often there is no follow-up activity. At the same time, action which feeds into frenetic busyness is counter-productive. As Green warns:

> Many parish churches overwhelm themselves with actions, meetings and projects that are not necessarily directed by careful theological reflection, and may in fact be a squandering of energies and resources rather than a faithful commitment to engage incarnationally with God in the world. Commitment is the adventure of faithful action, but engaging in any old action can be the outcome of frenzied excitability or frustration, derived from an inner anxiety about needing to be useful rather than an adventurous risk based upon a determination to engage in Kingdom

issues. We are not called to fritter our lives away but to risk them faithfully – and the (pastoral) cycle gives our action this quality.[8]

At this juncture, images can be used to provide a visual mission statement for planning and action. These images can be compared with those chosen in the *See* stage in order to clarify the steps that are needed to move from 'how we are now' to 'what we want to be and do'. Questions in the planning stage could include:

- How does our story relate to the Jesus story as portrayed in the pictures?
- In the light of our learning from the cycle, what does God want of us?
- What are the kingdom issues with which we need to engage?

In planning a strategy for action, both short-term and long-term goals need to be identified together with a timescale which will ensure accountability in realizing the goals. The 'who, why, what, when, where, and how' questions are a vital component in ensuring the smooth running of the process. Dates are set at regular intervals to assess progress. A Gateshead team ministry had their action plan as a fixed item on their PCC agenda. This allowed them to monitor progress and to keep their churches fully informed. Sustaining interest is a critical part of the process.

However, this is not the end of the process, because it is continuous. Confidence gained in having achieved certain goals, however modest they might be, provides the motivation for a new round of the *See, Judge, Act* cycle. The life and mission of the faith community is once again put under the spotlight so that further kingdom issues can be explored and addressed.

In an adaptation of the pastoral cycle, a youth group in St John the Evangelist Church in Birtley, in the north of Durham Diocese, used images of Christ in deciding on how to invest their precious savings of £80.00. Led by Brenda Jones, an experienced Mission Enabler (now a priest), the youngsters, aged between thirteen and seventeen, worked with two pictures in order to formulate ethical criteria in selecting a bank. First, they held a brainstorming session to reflect on how they saw Jesus at the present time. They then divided into two groups, one being given *The Laughing Christ* (*The Christ We Share*, no. 1), the other *The Angry Christ* (*The Christ We Share*, no. 9). Using these images, they were asked to discuss:

- What do you like or dislike about the image? What surprises you about it?

- What does it communicate to you about Christ?

- How does it compare with your original image of Jesus?

Those working with *The Laughing Christ* felt that God does not will suffering and that even in the midst of oppression there can be joy. Quoting the Beatitudes in Luke's Gospel, that 'those who weep today will laugh tomorrow' (6.21), they thought that change was already taking place; but wondered how the powerful, who expect the poor to weep, would account for their laughter. The other group had no problem in equating the anger of Christ with an unfair, unequal world, and with the way people's lives are manipulated by forces outside their control. They could identify with this experience themselves. Reflecting on these insights, the whole group was then asked what questions they would like to ask the banks before opening an account. They came up with the following:

- What is the policy of your bank on reducing Third World debt?

- Does your bank loan money to organizations involved in selling arms?

- How does your bank support the care of the environment?

The same letter was sent to all the banks in town but only one took it seriously. The manager admitted ignorance and the need to consult a senior colleague. A formal reply was eventually sent answering all the youngsters' queries. This process enabled them to become involved in ongoing discussions and to realize that in some small way they had power to challenge the status quo. For those who feel overwhelmed by powerlessness, this was a major step forward. Other banks either did not bother to reply or else sent a standard pack of information as to how to open an account. Not surprisingly, the Birtley youth group opted for the first bank and reported back to the parish their reasons for doing so.

The missiological challenge in many, if not most, churches is to change direction from forever looking inward and being locked in maintenance or inherited mode, to looking out to witness to the gospel imperatives of justice, peace and reconciliation. Using images of Christ to help people reflect theologically on the *missio Dei* can be far more effective than words alone in inspiring responsible action. The central message of every image is the good news of God's gift of transformed life in Christ, who is the paradigm of our transformation. It is God's will that we experience this new life through grace. No matter what the context, working with images offers a unique way of developing an authentic engaged spirituality which enables people to move forward in transforming themselves, their faith community, and the world around them.

❋ ❋ ❋ ❋ ❋

Exercises for reaching people on the edge

10. Bible studies and teaching

10.1 Titles for Christ

10.1.1 Consequences

- The group is divided into twos and threes. A number of images are passed round in succession. Each cluster decides on a snappy title or caption for the image. This is written down on the piece of paper accompanying each picture, folded over, and passed on, as in the game of Consequences.

- When all the pictures have circulated, compare the titles. Discuss similarities and differences.

- There are no right or wrong answers. Different people see different things in the same image. We learn from each other's perceptions, allowing our understanding of Jesus to grow.[9]

10.1.2 Biblical titles for Jesus

- Working in pairs, see how many biblical titles for Jesus you can recall. Make a list, e.g. Bread of Life, Light of the World, Messiah, Son of David, the Way, Saviour, Lamb of God, Logos, the Good Shepherd, Comforter, the New Adam, the True Vine, etc. Compare lists in a plenary group.

- There are about 200 such titles in the New Testament. When understood in their original context, they show what people saw in Jesus.

- Ask participants to find an image which matches one of the titles. Discuss.

- See **9.2** for **Titles for Christ in other cultures**

10.1.3 Titles for Jesus in hymns and choruses

- This exercise is done in small groups. Provide both old and modern hymnals. These can be from different denominations and traditions. Everyone can work on a mixture of old and modern hymns and choruses, or half the group can discuss older material and half modern. Carols can also be used.

- See how many titles for Jesus can be found in older hymnals and list them on large sheets of paper. Note how many times each title is used as evidence of its popularity, and the date of the hymnal.

- See how many titles for Jesus can be found in modern hymnals or chorus books and list them. Again, note the date and how many times each title is used.

- Display the lists where they can be seen. Identify significant differences in the use of titles for Jesus over the years and variations in popularity.

- Discussion questions:
  * What have been the most popular titles over time?
  * Why do you think some titles have been more popular than others at different times? What are the reasons for the changes in popularity?
  * What do contemporary titles for Jesus in hymns and choruses tell us about people's faith today?
  * Can we identify a different usage of titles for Jesus in different denominations and traditions? E.g. Catholic, Evangelical, Charismatic, Black Pentecostal, Methodist, Reformed, Baptist.
  * What do we think about the differences in usage?
  * Which is our favourite title, and why?

- This exercise is linked with images of Christ by trying to find pictures which resonate with the most popular titles over time. These images are then used as an aid to further discussion.

10.2 Bible studies using images of Christ

(Bibles are needed)

10.2.1 'I am Sayings'

Jesus made several statements which begin with 'I am ...' Look up the references in John's Gospel and complete the sentences. Jesus said:

- I am .... John 6.35   (the bread of life)
- I am .... John 8.12   (the light of the world)
- I am .... John 10.7   (the door of the sheep)
- I am .... John 10.11   (the good shepherd)
- I am .... John 11.25   (the resurrection)
- I am .... John 14.6   (the way, the truth and the life)
- I am .... John 15.1   (the true vine)

- Younger participants can draw pictures of the different 'I am ...' sayings followed by a discussion of what they mean.
- Participants can look for relevant pictures in a display of images. Discuss the implications of Jesus' use of this imagery as found in different contexts and cultures.[10]

10.2.2 If you had to preach a sermon on Christ, which text would you choose?

Personal work – the outcome of this can be shared in pairs

- Choose your text. How does it match the image/s you chose in the basic exercise?
- Is there any tension between your text and the image you selected?
- If so, can you locate the source of this tension and see how it can be resolved? Do you need to choose another image or another text?
- While we need a Jesus of history, we also need a Christ of a living faith who speaks to us today. How do you, or would you, live out the Christology expressed in your text together with your chosen image/s?

Group work – plenary

- Which were the most popular themes chosen by the group, and why?
- Is there a bias towards 'nurture', or 'challenge', in the chosen texts and images? Discuss the implications of any differences.

10.2.3 Matching gospel passages to images

- Each person is given an image of Christ and asked to find a relevant gospel passage to match the image.

- This is a fun exercise for those who are not so confident in finding their way around the Bible, and is best done in pairs so that people can help one another.

- After a specified time, the group shares their findings in turn. Other Scripture passages can be suggested for study, providing a further learning experience.

10.2.4 Exploring gospel themes using images

- Images are selected to portray different gospel themes and used as a basis for theological reflection, discussion, teaching or preaching preparation:
  * E.g. Advent, the Nativity, baptism of Christ, Christ in the wilderness, Lent, Passiontide, Good Friday, Easter, resurrection appearances, The Emmaus Road, Ascensiontide, etc.;
  * Christ's ministry of healing and teaching, sharing and celebrating;
  * The parables;
  * Being disciples of Christ – called and sent;
  * Christ with different people – Mary and Martha, the woman at the well, children, Zacchaeus, Nicodemus, Peter, the woman taken in adultery, the rich young man, etc ...;
  * Forgiveness, suffering, reconciliation, anger of Christ, justice.

- Depending on the theme, participants can be asked to find relevant passages in the Bible to increase their familiarity followed by a discussion. This is a useful starter for a teaching session.

10.3   Teaching about Christ

- The facilitator, minister or other teacher can follow the above exercises with a teaching session on Christ, or a whole series of teaching sessions or sermons.

- In a small group, images can be used as a visual aid to reflect on different aspects of the gospel story, or to clarify different aspects of faith. Beware of using theological jargon.

- At no time should participants be belittled or criticized for what they have shared. Working with images should always be an empowering exercise, giving people confidence in articulating and sharing their faith.

- Questions raised during an exercise are a good point of entry in teaching: starting where people are rather than where we think they should be, and then moving them on to a greater understanding.

11. Faith sharing

11.1 Reflecting on our own journey of faith

Following on from the basic exercise in Chapter 1, choose an image of **'Who was Christ for me as a child – or before my confirmation, ordination, marriage, tertiary education, or other significant event?'**

- Allow time for meditating on the image.

- Share in pairs as before.

- Compare your image with the one/s chosen in the basic exercise. Identify any significant changes in your faith as exemplified in the images:
  - * Do you think the changes signify a growth in faith?
  - * If so, what form has this taken?
  - * If there is no change and you have chosen the same or a similar image both times, do you think you are stuck in a rut?
  - * Reflections can be shared in the large group if this is helpful.
  - * If you were to choose an image which would be popular in your group or church, how would it differ from your own image? If the difference is quite considerable how would you resolve the tension? What would you do or say?

11.2 Sharing my own personal image of Christ

- People are invited to bring one or more images of Christ of their own, which have a special meaning to them, to the workshop. These may be paintings, carvings, pictures in a book or Bible, postcards, banners, crosses or crucifixes, etc. The art section in the local library is a useful resource.

- Sitting in a circle, group members take turns in sharing:
  - * Why the image is important to him or her.
  - * Who Christ is for them in the image.

- This is a good way of getting people to share their personal faith story. Allow plenty of time. Participants should be listened to respectfully and in silence, without comment except appreciation for the sharing. This can be an emotive experience but tears can be a healing part of the process.

- If the group agrees, questions can be asked at the end but no one should be forced to share anything against their wishes.

- This session can be followed by a shorter version of the Basic Exercise with images brought by the group providing a pooled resource for faith sharing. This is helpful when the group doesn't have access to other images, or has only a limited number available.

11.3   What aspects of Christ's character would I like to be seen in me?

- Decide on one aspect as listed below:
    * A friend to others no matter who they are.
    * Available when needed.
    * Compassionate and empathetic.
    * Never afraid to speak my mind and be prophetic.
    * Prepared to take risks whatever the personal cost.
    * Forgiving others who have wronged me.
    * Accepting people just as they are.
    * Working alongside the poor and the powerless.
    * Prepared to fight for justice and truth.

Choose an image which reflects your chosen aspect and share with a partner. (Obviously you can add to the above list.)

11.4   How do we live our faith in Christ?

- Why do you identify Jesus in the way you do?
- What difference does this, or could this, make in your life?
- How could you share your understanding of Jesus with others, such as your family, friends, workmates, colleagues?
- What image of Christ would help in this sharing?

11.5   Who is Jesus for those around us?

- What do people say about Jesus – family, friends, colleagues, people in your faith community or church, non-Christians, etc.?
- Why do they say this?
- What image of Jesus might change their perception?

12. Mission

12.1 Which image provides a visual mission statement of our faith community/church/group?

Typical groups include a confirmation class, parish away day, women's or men's group, all-age group, Sunday school, youth group, school or college group, older people's fellowship, homeless people, HIV/AIDS support group, hospice carers, ecumenical group, Bible study or home group, cell church, prayer fellowship, choir, servers, lay ministers, clergy chapter, deanery synod, Mothers' Union meeting, shared ministry team, fellowship for vocation, ordination candidates and post-ordination training, industrial mission, army, prison and student chaplaincies.

For further information see pages 55-56 in 'Mission on the home front', and pages 57-59 in 'Action stations with images' above.

13. Evangelism

13.1 Faith-sharing and witnessing

- The basic exercise is excellent in helping people to share their faith in a non-judgemental and affirming context.

- The mission exercise above takes this a step further in enabling people to be more forceful in witnessing to their faith in a friendly and fun environment. Both exercises are an ideal way of building up people's confidence in talking about Christ to family and friends, colleagues and workmates, those of uncertain faith and those with none.

13.2 Persuaders

This is a more overtly evangelistic exercise:

- The images are set out on display. Each person chooses a picture. They then try to convince someone else that theirs is the best image of Jesus, giving their reasons. If they convince someone, they then pair off to persuade someone else. After 10 to 15 minutes see how many groups have formed.

What picture has the most followers and why?

Reflection in small groups

What factor most influenced you in your final choice of picture?

- * the arguments of the advocates?
- * the enthusiasm of the advocates?
- * the number of the advocates?

* the persuasive power of the group leader?
* the picture itself?
* loyalty to friends?
* anything else?

- Did the argument for a particular picture change in the course of the activity?

- Did anyone change their choice of picture more than once? If so, how easy was it to make changes? What influenced them?

- Did the exercise have anything to say about the way we present Jesus to others either in preaching, conversation, or simply in the images we use in church or Sunday school?

- How did people feel about taking part in the exercise? Positive and negative feelings need to be explored.

- Discuss how this exercise could be used with other groups. Would it be necessary to adapt it in any way for other contexts?[11]

4

Moving Beyond Words

'A woolly idea of God'

In north-east England there is a widespread belief in God, not necessarily a Christian God but definitely English, while popular religion largely ignores Jesus. This deity is generally thought to care for people in good times and in bad. Women, especially, speak of having experienced God's protection in answer to prayer; and this evidence is reinforced by fieldwork studies.

In a survey done by a small group of women parishioners on a deprived Stockton-on-Tees estate, they found that 'more people believed in God than would admit to it. He is something they keep in the cupboard, and say, "When I need God he will be there and I will go and tell him my troubles. But while everything is going fine I don't need him." ' Such an attitude was as prevalent among churchgoers as non-churchgoers. As Pauline explained: 'He is a Comfort God, a Panic-Button God. When you push the panic button he is expected to jump forward. No problem. I'll sort all this out, I'll do this and that. And after the panic is over they shove him back and say thank you very much. Next time I need you I'll give you a call.' The prevailing belief is that, in a crisis, God will send someone or do something to fix the problem. This is exemplified in Edna's

story, except that for her, a faithful parishioner in Hartlepool, God was a living reality:

I am disabled and can only walk outside with a stick or holding on to someone's arm. One morning, when I was coming home after shopping, I found that the road I had to cross had been dug up by workmen and was all rubble. I had a shopping bag over my left arm, a carrier bag in my left hand and my stick in the right one, and I didn't know how I was going to cross over. I looked both ways to see if there was anyone coming who could help, but there wasn't a soul about. So I started to cross, but I knew I couldn't make it. I heard myself say out loud, 'Please, God, help me.' I felt a lovely warm feeling pass through my body and heard a voice say, 'Give me your bags, Luv, and hold my arm.'

I felt rooted to the spot because only minutes before there had been no one about. I believe that it was the lovely warm feeling that helped me to turn round. I saw a young man standing there and his face seemed to glow. I knew that God was with us. I said, 'Have you jumped from Heaven?' He laughed and said 'No.

I've jumped from my cab,' and he pointed over the road to where one of those huge lorries with the cab very high up was standing. He said he had been sitting in the cab having his lunch when he saw me look both ways and felt I needed help. I went straight home and prayed for him. I felt he was really good, the way he came to help me. No one would have known if he hadn't bothered, except God. Thanks be to God.

There is also a strongly held belief in a supernatural divine mechanism that is going to judge either for or against you, and that when things go wrong it is your due – 'Trials are sent to try us.' It is even thought that some sort of spiritual force may actually conspire against you – 'I will be glad when this year is over. Three bad things have happened to curse the year. In the new year there is a chance of things going right again.' This fatalistic attitude spills over into the National Lottery, supported by a supernatural conviction that 'you are either meant to win or you are not. And it must be right if you win'. Lottery advertising has played on this belief with a big, sparkling finger promising untold riches, pointing directly at people out of the heavens.

Although the people in the Stockton survey were said to have 'a woolly idea of God', what impressed the women's group was the number of non-churchgoers who lived their life 'in a good Christian way': 'They do their work outside the church, amongst other people. People you don't even know talk to you and tell you things,

open their hearts to you. It's God's way, isn't it? That's God. The open mind and the open heart. He works through people, even those who don't go to church.'

A group of professional people in a picturesque village on the banks of the River Tees maintained that rural people pray only to God; and that in their worship of God the loving Father they have no desire to know Christ for themselves. However, for children from broken homes, a Father God would be problematic, for many do not know their fathers – 'My father never comes to see me' – and some of them may be in prison.

One person suggested that in a former coal-mining society, God would be seen by non-churchgoers as the all-powerful Mine Manager, or even the more distant owner, while Jesus would be regarded as one of the bosses, 'not one of the lads like us'. But for a miner's widow, who is a regular churchgoer, God is 'a big friend. Somebody to lean on and get power from'. Here, in imaging God a distinction is made between spiritual power, available to all, and the controlling power of class in what was once a rigidly stratified feudal society.

For many in some northern communities, God is seen as an authority figure, the all-powerful voice in the sky. But, while God is far removed, Jesus is seen as being more accessible and caring: 'All the children are brought up on Jesus being born in a stable. This is what they learn in school. Knowing that Jesus was a baby makes them think he is more like them.' This explains something of the popularity of crib and Christingle services, when churches are full. For adult church members, Jesus is quintessentially the Good Shepherd, for the rest, a handy expletive.

In an informal survey of a suburban area of Stockton, the concept of Jesus as Saviour of the world was common among those who had links with their evangelical parish church. A newly confirmed woman, who had come to church after her husband's death, gave her testimony: 'Jesus is God's only son. He came to earth to help us. He suffered and died for us. Jesus is with us always. He knows our pain and suffering, as well as our happiness. Jesus is with us when we call out to him. He is a constant support and help to all.' But a 17-year-old, who had had a church upbringing but left after her father's death, would have none of this:

> I don't know if there is a God and I don't care. Because all religions are just an excuse not to question the evil in the present world, but promise a better world after this one. Jesus is an historical figure, who may have lived around the time of the Roman occupation of the Middle East. I think he or someone like him did good work to help the poor and ill.

In a deprived estate on the banks of the Tees, many people are confronted daily by the grimness and difficulties of their lives, lurching from crisis to crisis that include attempted suicide, rape, incest, schoolgirl pregnancies, serious illness, drug and alcohol abuse, vandalism, violence and trouble with the police. Yet for them, God is loving and caring, and the people are generally loving and caring towards each other. Anyone in trouble is looked after. This is a mostly lapsed Catholic community and even though they no longer have a church, 'God is alive and well.' Two nuns living there noted that people love prayers indicating that God is with them, giving them hope. Jesus and the cross are included in their devotions, and Easter services in the community centre are well attended.

People on the estate have their own religious imagery. Many carry a much-fingered embroidered 'Cross in my Pocket', as a talisman. Plastic-coated prayer cards are given at times of bereavement. These people firmly believe that the dead are in God's care in heaven. There is no concept of hell in the afterlife. Hell is right here on earth and it is those who are left behind who suffer misery. Because they connect people to God, prayer cards are thought to be infused with spiritual power, offering tangible protection. Cards with crosses are popular as are Dürer's 'Praying Hands'. Favourite poems include 'Footprints', 'If', 'The Sand Dollar Legend', 'The Gate of the Year', and 'Death is nothing at all': 'I have only slipped away into the next room. Whatever we were to each other, that we still are ... I am waiting for you, for an interval, somewhere very near, just around the corner. All is well.'

Prayers tell us a lot about the pressing anxieties of people and their faith. During the late 1990s, Raymond Dick, vicar of Harton St Peter in South Shields, spent an afternoon a week with a couple of lay people covering his parish street by street asking for prayer requests. They were seldom rejected. Health problems featured prominently in the petitions as did concern for both the bereaved and the departed. Family troubles were another recurring theme as were security and finding a job, reflecting the tough lives of the locals. More surprisingly, prayer requests for world peace surfaced regularly, since this was during the Bosnian war.

An analysis of prayers, written by a broader cross-section of people visiting the 'Faith Worth Sharing' exhibition in Durham Cathedral during the summer of 1993, yielded similar themes. The majority of contributors clearly believed in an all-powerful and caring God, a Mr Fix-It who could put things to rights. Once more, sickness, bereavement and loss dominated the petitions. In an anthology compiled by Philip Thomas, theologian and vicar of Heighington St Michael, a child sends kisses for God to pass on to Grandpa, while others of the departed are asked if they are having a nice time and whether they have met up in heaven.

The bulk of the remaining concerns revolved around the fragility of relationships, family responsibilities, crises in decision-making, anxieties about jobs and unemployment, threats to young people, animals, and world peace. My favourite reads: 'Dear God, as far as I (and any intelligent person) can see, you do not exist. So will you please stop pretending you do – and stop hassling me.' Thomas notes that many saw prayers as an answering service, while for others, it was

a direct line to God. Summarizing the petitions, he concludes that 'it is to a cry of pain, an appeal for meaning, a shout for justice, or just occasionally a longing for God, that an answer must be given'.[1] As much as we would want to find God in the world around us as we reach out in mission, the immediacy of pain and suffering cannot be ignored and needs pastoring.

This brief overview of concepts of God and Christ in the North East, impressionistic as it is, shows the importance of taking popular beliefs seriously in different contexts. But while we cannot point to the visible presence of God, and must accept living with uncertainty, Christians are assured that Christ is the human face of God and it is through Christ that we come to know him. In reflecting on images of Christ, it is amazing how people who would normally struggle to express their beliefs, surprise even themselves with the theological depth of their observations.

Hide-and-seek with spirituality

Like 'mission', 'spirituality' is a slippery term with a thousand different definitions depending on your religious bias. My difficulty in Durham was in coming to a working understanding of spirituality in a church that covers the full range of Anglican traditions, with a charismatic wing thrown in for good measure, and not forgetting a vibrant folk spirituality which underlies and permeates all the rest.

The Durham theologian, Stephen Barton, defines the essence of Christian spirituality as being twofold: 'the sense of the divine presence and living in the light of that presence'. He clarifies these two basic aspects as 'knowing and being known by God, on the one hand, and responding with the whole of life, on the other'.[2] In practice this means that 'spirituality has to do with life under God: and for Christians, it has to do specifically with life under the God who is revealed in Jesus and who graces believers with the Spirit'.[3]

In my experience, spirituality was more usually expressed in the first half of the definition, 'sensing the divine presence' through prayer and communion with God. The second clause, about living God's love through 'responding with the whole of life', received short shrift in much parish ministry. The gospel story is a story of the divine presence living in the midst of God's people. This is what the good news is about. Obviously you live in the light of the presence when you actually witness to the presence which lived in our midst (cf. John 1.10).

I believe that we are called to integrate the inner dynamic of creative love, inspired by sustained communion with God, with an outer compulsion to engage in the transformation of people and society. Naturally, transformation has social, political and economic implications as well as spiritual ones. In a pastoral letter issued by the 1988 Lambeth Conference 'On the Gospel and Transformation', transformation is described as the theological linchpin which holds inner personal change and socio-political change firmly together 'in one Gospel and one witness in the One Body'.[4] This means that an authentic engaged spirituality cannot be divorced from the real world, from injustice, suffering and oppression; and that it finds expression in respecting the human dignity of, and having compassion for, each and every person through the love of God.

This is a far cry from the findings of David Hay and Kate Hunt of the University of Nottingham in their in-depth study of 'the spiritual life of people who don't go to church'.[5] This is analogous with the north-eastern experience except that there it could include churchgoers. Using national surveys as their starting point, they note that 'slightly more than 76 per cent of the national population are now likely to admit to having had a spiritual or religious experience'. This figure signifies an almost 60 per cent rise over the past thirteen years. In its broadest terms the religious experience would embrace the following:

- consciousness of a transcendent providence seemingly influencing one's life pattern;

- awareness of the presence of God both in times of distress and contentment;

- conviction of prayer being answered especially in a crisis situation;

- a sense of a sacred presence in nature;

- a feeling of communing with the departed;

- foreboding of an evil entity.[6]

Hay and Hunt deduce that the dramatic increase in spiritual awareness may well be more to do with a greater openness to talk about religion in postmodern society than about any actual growth in such experience. Even so, the fact that most people surveyed had either rejected the Church or had never had any contact with it, underscores the conscious search of many for a spirituality that makes sense of their lives. The quest for self-empowerment is frequently directed towards a plethora of New Age resources and self-fulfilment courses, which offer a broad range of choice. In contrast, the Church is widely seen as being spiritually impoverished, busy peddling dry dogma and doctrine without opening up channels of direct encounter with God.

Even among regular churchgoers there is a tendency towards a personal spirituality. A religious pluralism in which church belonging is maintained independently of spiritual fulfilment is as common in Europe as it is south of the Equator. In Africa, a mission church member would resolve this dichotomy by visiting a traditional doctor (*inyanga*) or seer (*sangoma*), or attending a healing service in an African indigenous church at night and in secret, in addition to formal Sunday worship. In Britain, colour therapy, channelling, spiritualism, faith healing, astrology, an anger-release workshop, courses for self-enlightenment or getting in touch with the inner man or woman, or the ritual care of a grave can fulfil the same functions among churchgoers.

This is a sad indictment of the Church's inability to satisfy people's spiritual hunger, especially in worship. What is worrying is not the Church's unwillingness to nurture people spiritually but its apparent impotence in fostering a desire to encounter God. Of even greater concern is that it fails to acknowledge such deficiencies. Instead, the Church seeks to impose a formal, institutionalized spirituality to meet either the perceived, or the prescribed, needs of the people of God, hindering them from discovering an authentic spirituality, which they can make their own, within the rich heritage of the Christian tradition (cf. Matthew 23.13). You cannot live by somebody else's faith. One has to find one's own personal faith, and such a discovery comes through holy listening to God.

Retreats and workshops dedicated to contemplative spirituality draw increasingly on the writing and practices of the Christian mystics, but the financial cost involved and the pervasive cerebral ethos can make this rather exclusive. More challenging is the fact that the meditation industry tends to flourish in a contextual vacuum. As Jay Kothare, Anglican priest with a wealth of inner-city experience in England and Canada, maintains, 'Any spirituality of prayer or contemplation which is not rooted in a struggle for justice and equality is a pseudo spirituality, no matter how exotic or holy'.[7] For the sake of credibility in a world riven by inequality and poverty, the Church urgently needs to rediscover a mode of meditation which takes into account our Christian vocation to be co-workers with Christ in bringing in the kingdom. But first, we need a deeper understanding of the folk spirituality which pervades English Christianity.

Folk religion as inculturation

Whatever term is used, whether it be folk, implicit or popular religion, it continues to flourish despite concerted attempts in the Church to either ignore, condemn, control or suppress it, for this is what inculturation is all about. It is not something new, relating to some postmodern subculture, which can be manipulated by the Church. People have been translating the gospel into different forms in different contexts over the centuries, and will continue to do so as they seek to make sense of new challenges in their lives. A case in point is a Mothering Sunday service in a working class area in Stockton-on-Tees.

It was shortly after the Dunblane tragedy and people throughout the country had been asked to observe a minute's silence at 9.30 a.m., no matter where they were, as is the custom in times of national mourning or remembrance. In the parish concerned the weekly Eucharist started at 9.15 a.m. The small congregation asked that the minute's silence be observed on time. The priest brushed this aside, saying that prayers would be offered for Dunblane during the intercessions. As it was Mothering Sunday, he had designed a special liturgy with what he thought were appropriate symbols for a deprived area, such as a girl coming forward with a mop and bucket. Liturgical imperatives meant that no silence was kept at any point during the service.

The congregation was devastated. Most were unemployed and with a high mortality rate in their area, and this national tragedy had brought their own suffering into stark relief. Not only were they denied an opportunity to express solidarity with a grieving community, but they were not given a chance to address the gnawing questions of their own lives in any sort of meaningful imagery and ritual. They felt hurt, too, that in commemorating the death and resurrection of Christ in the Eucharist, no link had been made with the tragic death of the children at Dunblane. Some contemplated leaving the church.

Class and education were factors here. They said of the priest, 'He doesn't speak our language.' Too often middle-class values determine the aesthetics of taste and political correctness in the Church heritage industry, whether it is in tombstones and their inscriptions, flower arrangements, religious artefacts, music, language, liturgy or doctrine. The implicit spirituality of folk religion with its homespun imagery and symbols of identity and belonging, which have arisen over time out of shared values and experience, are thus excluded. The faithful worshippers might well suffer 'religious schizophrenia', being alienated from their inherent symbolic consciousness, while marginal and disinterested people are distanced from the Church by an unbridgeable chasm of mutual income-prehension.

The folk spirituality implicit in memorial shrines commemorating death on the roads, with their crosses, inscriptions and flowers, do not impinge directly on the life of the Church, but the death of Diana, Princess of Wales, was a big challenge up north. Whereas in the south, flowers and books of remembrance were more commonly set up in supermarkets and shopping malls, in the north, churches had to remain open to receive mountains of flowers, toys, letters, cards, messages in memorial books, and the prayers of many people. Elaborate shrines were fashioned with photos of the 'people's princess' flanked by flowers and lighted candles, while soft music played in the background. People in the north east are visual and the imagery and rituals of folk religion found expression in a tremendous outpouring of sentiment and sympathy, reinforced by a shared sense of loss.

The Big Meeting Day or Miners' Gala (Gayla) held annually each July in Durham, is a coming together of politics and folk religion. When it began in 1981 it was political, a demonstration of solidarity by miners in their struggle for just employment, but it evolved into a major event. Shops were boarded up as miners and their families streamed into the city by bus and train to listen to the impassioned oratory of leading Liberal and Labour politicians. Anti-establishment both in religion and politics, the solidarity of northern socialism yet retains a religious component as found in the miners' banners and the cathedral service.

In the early days, each Lodge of the more than a hundred Durham pits had its distinctive banner, a symbol of identity and belonging. As a miner said, 'The banner was the heart of your pit, and you followed the banner to the Big Meeting.'

Most sported political or socialist themes, but a good number were religious, much influenced by the Primitive Methodism of chapel folk. Lumley Colliery's first banner used a gospel text to critique the infamous Bond whereby pitmen were the chattels of wealthy mine owners: 'Stand fast therefore in the liberty wherewith Christ hath made you free, and be not entangled with the yoke of bondage.' Elsewhere, the faggot (symbolizing binding and strength), the wheatsheaf and the widow's mite stood alongside portraits of political prodigies and Union pioneers. Others bore images of the Good Samaritan, Jesus with children or calming the storm, and Durham Cathedral. In an agnostic pragmatism typical of pitmen, Karl Marx and Arthur Cook might front the banner, while Jesus and the angels graced the back.

Durham has long been revered as the capital of the coalfields, the cathedral standing as the Christian symbol of the north east, even among agnostics, despite the 'town and gown' image of the ancient university and the Church of England's shameful history as a mine owner. One mine was called 'Dean and Chapter', while the Dean was dunked in the River Wear during a 1920s Gala in the mistaken belief that he was Bishop Hensley Henson. Nonetheless, there is an impressive miners' memorial in the cathedral and the special service that has ended the Gala since 1987 is a moving experience as the joyous multitude follow their bands and banners across the Wear and up the narrow streets into the cathedral. Each year three pits are selected to lead the service and their villagers proudly process behind their banners accompanied by booming brass bands. Following pit closures, the Gala is now a modest affair but still arouses deep emotions. St Cuthbert's shrine is situated beyond the cathedral's high altar and 'Cuddies' people', as they are known, see the Gala service as an annual pilgrimage.

Pilgrimage is another symbolic ritual in the north in which folk spirituality and formal religion are inextricably entwined. People celebrate the spiritual riches of their ancient Celtic past, while people in Durham parishes regularly visit the cathedral to celebrate the lives of St Cuthbert and the Venerable Bede, whose shrine is in the Galilee chapel. Pilgrimages to sacred places like Lindisfarne Holy Island, Jarrow, Whitby, Walsingham and the northern abbeys and cathedrals are integral to parish life. For the pilgrims, the coach journey, communal singing, sharing of food, ritual observances associated with particular sites, and sacramental worship, all add to an intense spiritual experience. Bottles of blessed water, religious pictures, rosaries, badges, and other sacred mementoes are ways of reclaiming something of the numinous pilgrimage experience later within the drabness and drudgery of what is so often daily life.

Doreen recalls the spiritual highs of an annual parish pilgrimage to Walsingham:

It's lovely, a little bit of heaven. We have a short service on the coach and then start singing our hymns and old songs like 'Pack up your troubles'. As we get near we sing the Ave Maria, the Walsingham hymn. When you get off the coach everything just leaves you. We go to the different services, the altars dedicated to various saints, and the Holy House of our Lady of Walsingham, with all the beautiful candles. At the end you go down to the well and the priests bless you with holy water. I put it on my neck because I had thyroid trouble, and walk in puddles of water for my bad feet. Everyone wants you to bring holy water back with you. If they are sick they drink it, or else they put it on a painful place. Visiting holy places builds feeling of religion up and gives you strength to do the work of the church.

Clearly, the innate spirituality of folk religion, with its rich storehouse of imagery and symbols, cannot be separated out from formal Christian belief and practice. It is deeply ingrained within the life and soul of good and faithful churchgoers throughout the country, nourishing them spiritually and giving their life added meaning. Our challenge is to value the creative, and provide opportunities for people to grow in a lasting faith that is founded on the love of Christ. This is where meditating with images of Christ can offer a measure of discernment and provide a sure foundation for transformation.

Meditating with images

The Bible tells us, 'Be still and know that I am God' (Psalm 46.10). Reams have been written about the need for prayer and meditation in cultivating a real and deeply personal relationship with God, and of the importance of stillness and silence in order that we might 'hear God's voice in our lives and the will of God working in the world'.[8] For Mark Dyer, Episcopal American bishop, 'Silence is the language of God. Everything else is a bad translation.' But how, in the frenetic busyness of our lives, or in a culture that is saturated with noise and words, are we able to be still and find silence, to move beyond doing to being?

De Mello's observation that 'people feed on words, live by words, would fall apart without them'[9] is as true of the Church as of individuals. In his regular *Church Times* column, Simon Parke comments wryly about Anglican silence:

> Whereby the vicar announces a time for reflection merely in order to give himself time to look for his sermon notes, or to change the batteries in his faltering battery mike. Or worse, he announces a silence, the congregation breathe a sigh of relief, and then he proceeds to talk all the way through it, telling everyone how long it will be, and then explaining what they should be doing with it, by which time it's the next hymn. Loud, and with eight very long verses.[10]

Countrywide, people are so conditioned to relentless activity that the effort to keep still for any length of time can also be very difficult. The relatively recent culture of mobile phones and text messages, and the use of personal stereos and iPods means that some people find silence threatening. This is where working with images of

Christ has been so successful in giving people a way in to meditation. Initially they have something to hold, to look at, and to think about. Only later do they let go of the images to journey more deeply inwards in the presence of God.

In meditating on an image, one enters into the dynamics of some aspect of the gospel story as depicted in the picture. It is a highly personal experience as one becomes a character in the story and completes the picture for oneself. Indeed, artists sometimes include themselves in their paintings as their special signature. Incarnational meditation differs only from conventional meditation in that it begins by focusing on portrayals of the incarnate Son of God in and through different stages of his earthly ministry and beyond. The basic technique for both is the same.[11]

In preparing to meditate it is important to choose a comfortable physical posture using cushions, a prayer stool or chair. The spine needs to be straight, hands gently placed in the lap unless holding a picture, and shoulders relaxed. Some training may be needed to help people adopt a particular posture without fidgeting as stillness is essential. The aim is not to induce a trance, or even total relaxation, because the whole purpose of meditating with images is to heighten one's awareness of the saving activity of the incarnation. One is not only meditating with mind and heart, but with one's whole being. It is a full-bodied contemplation of the mystery of the incarnation involving all our senses.

A consciously shared silence is integral to the process. It is a good idea to start with short periods of silence, and then slowly extend these times during the course of the exercise. People can be encouraged to find a quiet space alone in order to meditate; but this may be too challenging for some who prefer to be with others. Affirmation and encouragement are the most important aspects of any workshop.

In an incarnational meditation on an image, a participant can either reflect on an image by itself, or else on a scriptural text linked with the image. Hopefully this reflection will then be linked to the person's daily life and experience, so that it becomes a way of doing theology in their own context. In this exercise, the pictures engage a participant on three different levels:

Who is Christ for me? What do I feel or think about Christ?

Who am I in Christ? What do I feel or think about myself?

Who is Christ in me? What difference does he make in my life?

In the basic exercise (Chapter 1), we dealt with the participant's choice of an image and how that choice relates to one's relationship with, and understanding of, Christ. The second and third levels of questioning are a natural development of the exercise, challenging the participant to look at himself or herself. The enquiry into the nature of Christ is inextricably linked with the enquiry into one's own nature for one's understanding of Christ is inevitably informed by one's self-understanding. Here, Christology and psychology are interrelated. This mutuality is implied in Jesus' loaded question: 'Who do *you* say *I* am?' In this sense, working with the images unfailingly puts one in touch with oneself and that is why it is such an emotional experience for many people.

In reflecting on the saving grace of the living God, one is reflecting on one's own existential situation. You cannot possibly relate to God unless you have come to terms with your own spiritual destiny. On a personal journey, the revelation of a redeeming God flows in tandem with the equally indispensable revelation of the individual in need of redemption. So, in Matthew 16.13-19, Peter's identification of Jesus as the Christ is immediately followed by Jesus identifying Peter as the Rock. However, Jesus' identification of Peter does not cover the identity of other believers. Nor does Peter's discipleship prescribe the nature of ours. Every individual has a unique relationship with God. Peter only represents one kind of relationship with God, and one kind of response, mercifully allowing others to relate to him in many different ways.

When they meditate with images, people are empowered to do full justice to the reality of their personalities, and to be free to be themselves in the way they follow Christ. That is why working together as a group is so important in allowing one to validate both one's own and others' unique journeys. Listening with love is such an affirmation for people, for while it affirms us as individuals it also affirms the way we journey together. As Jesus said, 'For where two or three are gathered in my name, I am there among them' (Matthew 18.20). The more we fulfil our own individual destiny, the more we are at one with God.

After a time, the threefold enquiry, involving both discursive thinking and emotive response, should lead to a period of introspection and silence. Having let go of the feeling content of the image, such a silence offers us the opportunity to encounter the real presence of Christ in the depths of our being, the whole purpose of meditation. As Bede Griffiths explains:

> In meditation, we try to go beyond the limitation of words and thoughts to open our hearts to the hidden mystery of the Spirit and to be really in the presence of Christ and the Father, to enter into the mystery of the Trinity ... The Spirit is where we go beyond our ego, beyond the limited self, and open on to the divine, and meet the transcendent God. At that intersection of the Spirit God and the soul, the transcendent and the immanent meet.[12]

The hardest part in meditation is to still one's mind. John Main, who did so much to restore Christian meditation to its rightful place in the Church, compares the distracting chaos of the mind 'to a tree filled with chattering monkeys'.[13] Some people find the repetition of the Jesus Prayer ('Jesus Christ, Son of Mary, have mercy on me, a sinner' or merely 'Lord Jesus, have mercy'), co-ordinated with breathing, a help in stilling the mind and deepening the meditation. Others prefer the silent recitation of a short text from the Bible, a verse from the Psalms, or the repetition of a key phrase in the shape of a *mantra*. For John Main, a *mantra* works best in handling distractions, 'because the purpose of the one word is simply to bring your mind to peace, silence and concentration. Not to bring it to rest with holy thoughts alone but to transcend what we know as thought altogether. The mantra ... is like a plough that goes through your mind pushing everything else aside'.[14]

Mantras can be significant biblical names like Mary, Jesus, Christ; or words like Amen, Hosanna, Abba (Father), Emmanuel, Shalom; or phrases like Halleluiah, Maranatha (much favoured by John Main), 'I am that I am', Glory be, Hail Mary, Ave Maria, Kyrie (Christe) Eleison; or even imaginative invocations like 'Jesus save (heal, feed, protect) me', 'Come down, Holy Spirit', 'Come, Lord Jesus', 'Bless me, Lord', 'Thy will be done' or 'Thy Kingdom come'.

A rosary may be another aid in sustaining the flow of meditation. A wooden holding cross is yet another means of coming into the presence of Christ. Such a cross has an uneven transverse beam so that it fits comfortably between the fingers while being cradled in the palm of the hand. Holding the cross silently can in itself be a prayer. In addition, lighted candles in a darkened room, incense, joss sticks, sweetgrass, chanting and the playing of suitable music could further deepen the experience, but there needs to be common agreement in a group situation. What some people find helpful may be anathema to others. The leader needs to begin and end the meditation, perhaps with the ringing of a bell or the gentle striking of some other musical instrument. The timing of the meditation should also be made clear beforehand. It is helpful to leave the place of meditation in silence and to allow people time to surface from the depths of their experience.

Our fortnightly gatherings at Temenos offered a different model of incarnational meditation in that our regular meeting together not only helped to build up trust, so that our reflections were shared at an ever deepening level, but also extended the process of prayer and meditation to the days and weeks ahead. Reflecting on the experience, Billy Kennedy, spiritual director of Temenos, noted that many Christians are still fairly uncomfortable with the whole notion of meditation, believing it to be something exotic, if not actually forbidden. Our culture is largely to blame in that much of the literature revels in describing strange phenomena such as lights, colours and whispering voices. But what Kennedy appreciated was the essentially non-threatening way in which meditating with images allowed one to move beyond the world of ideas and exegesis into a deeper silence within oneself, and thus into a deeper experience of God. As he says:

> Meditation requires both a will and a surrendering, allowing the images to sink into the depth of one's being where the Holy Spirit 'does all the work'. A danger in some ways with personal spiritual endeavour, is that

many of us feel it has to be productive – we have to come away from our practices, prayer meetings and workshops having learnt more. Obviously there is nothing amiss in enriching and extending one's knowledge, and a great deal of Christian endeavour is as a result of being inspired in these ways. But one cannot but help have the sense that this is all just the moistening of the ground. The deeper invitation is always there too. Not only to be open to what God is personally saying to me, but to surrender, much like an image of the Rabbi who knowing the Torah by heart, leans his head against the Eastern wall, and gives over to silent love.[15]

In the extended process of incarnational meditation, time is put aside in the days that follow to return to one's reflections on an image. At some point, one might think that the subject has been exhausted, or become bored with it, or question its relevance in one's life. But according to Kennedy, this feeling of going up a blind alley is precisely the moment to keep going because this is when one can shift gears and enter into the rich life of contemplation:

> Our thoughts begin to sink into the unconscious, elaborating, connecting, developing. Sometimes they blossom into the unexpected insight, a subtle alteration of behaviour, a gradual but pervasive change of attitude. Indeed, the more my reflection on the joy of the Risen Christ becomes

part of my being, the more my whole days are lived in the light of it.[16]

In fact spiritual images of Christ, the apostles and saints have often been used in the Christian contemplative tradition as a focus for absorbing the desired qualities of that spiritual being. In this merging, a oneness is experienced with the image in a fusion of subject and object.

From a psychological point of view, the possibility exists that just because we do not know why we have chosen a certain image, the time may be ripe for the psyche to open out to the unconscious and to reveal untended and unhealed wounds. This may mean that much deeper and different levels are waiting to be explored; but this journey to healing and wholeness needs to be done safely, with an experienced companion, in the light of Christ. As one begins to move ever deeper into one's inner life, one is guided to bring the light of consciousness into the shadow areas so that one can begin to relate with love and understanding to the whole person I am.[17]

For centuries, Christian orthodoxy has used images to remind us of the qualities of the divine, and also to reveal to us that we are called to 'become Christ' in the world. 'That they may be one' takes on a deeper significance, as indeed does the invitation to 'be born again'. The aim of meditation is to marry independent theological reflection with a cultivated response from the heart, together with the full attunement and awareness of body and soul. Such an incarnational meditation should free us to go out into the world to fulfil the mission of God, passionate about sharing and living out our faith (cf. John 17.20-24). But listening to God must come first.

As Archbishop Desmond Tutu rightly says, we must follow Jesus' own example in which 'disengagement, waiting on God, precedes engagement'. Tutu believes that an authentic spirituality of transformation requires that we all become contemplatives: that we first have to spend time with Jesus in the wilderness before we can start dealing with issues of justice, peace and reconciliation. And then we must needs take the suffering of our wounded world back to God in prayer and contemplation.[18]

❋ ❋ ❋ ❋ ❋

Exercises for moving beyond words

14. Meditation

14.1 Meditating with images

For information on using images for an incarnational meditation, see above.

14.2   Meditating on an image of Christ (abridged and edited – source unknown)

St Paul calls Jesus 'the *image* of the invisible God' (Colossians 1.15): an image of Christ is an image of the Image.

- Open yourself to God's presence. Use a *breathing prayer*, e.g. 'Lord, that I may see!' Ask God to speak to you through an image of Christ.

- Look at the image carefully, exploring the details. Get to know the image. Get inside it.

- Now ask God to show you what this image tells you about him. Where is *he* in this image? *Why* is he there?

- Now look for yourself in the image. Which aspects of you are in this image? What does it tell you about yourself, your needs, worries, experiences? Try to make the connection.

- Of the many thoughts you have had, choose the one you regard as the most important. Thank God for it. Tell him why and how this 'thought' speaks to you of *him* and of *yourself*.

- A reflection: You are God's work of art, created in Christ Jesus to live the good life as from the beginning he intended us to live it (Ephesians 2.10).

15.   Prayer

The first step in deepening our spirituality is our relationship with Christ. One or more images of Christ may be used for prayer, meditation and worship.

15.1   Praying before an image of Christ

- Printed prayers on card or prayer manuals are provided as an aid to prayer.

- Paper and pencils are available so that people can write their own prayers and petitions. These can be offered up later in worship.

- The same procedure can be followed as in meditation.

15.2   Writing a letter to God

This can follow on from an exercise with images as a way of helping those who find prayer difficult, to express their innermost thoughts and feelings.

- The writer addresses a personal letter to God in a conversational style. This is best done at leisure and in private; but, provided sufficient time and space are available, it can take place during a workshop.

- The writer might like to discuss the letter with a spiritual director or minister afterwards.

15.3   Prayer and vocation

Images can be used by both lay people and clergy to reflect on their vocation, and to pray for discernment in knowing what direction God is calling them to go. This follows on well from the basic exercise. Sufficient time should be allowed for prayer and meditation, and silence is essential. Bibles are needed.

- Participants are asked to choose one or more images from a display and then meditate on the question: **Who am I in Christ now?**

- Bibles can be used as an aid to reflection.

- One image only is retained while any others are returned to the display before embarking on the next question: **Who is God calling me to be?**

- Again, Bibles are used for discernment in listening to God.

- Some people might wish to discuss their experience with a partner but others might prefer to remain silent, and should not be coerced into sharing. A time of prayer naturally follows, both as individuals and as a group. People might like to offer up their images to God in worship.

15.4   Setting aside a prayer space in church

- The space needs to be inviting with comfortable seating, a prayer desk, a cross or crucifix, Bibles, candles and a selection of images which are changed regularly. Images which highlight different liturgical seasons or follow a theme such as forgiveness and healing, justice and peace, bereavement, or care of the earth can be used intermittently to sustain interest.

- Prayer cards and manuals are provided. The various Mission Societies, Christian Aid and CAFOD all provide excellent free prayer resources as well as published collections of prayers from around the world.

- Setting time aside for regular group prayer encourages a disciplined life of witness for any faith community.

15.5   A prayer walk or pilgrimage route using images of Christ

- The pilgrimage route can be set up indoors or in the open, depending on the weather. Large images of Christ are placed at strategic points at each station. If outdoors, the images must be firmly secured and rainproofed. The aisles of a large church or cathedral are ideal if indoors. Whether inside or out seating should be provided at each station to encourage people to stop, meditate and pray.

- This works well when images from different countries are used together with prayers from those same places. USPG arranged such a pilgrimage route from Fountains Abbey to Ripon Cathedral in Yorkshire. Deer grazing in the meadows and fields ablaze with poppies added much to the experience. The stations were set out along winding paths in the abbey grounds; everyone received a map of the pilgrimage at the start. The pilgrimage began with a service in the abbey ruins and ended with a celebration in the cathedral using liturgical material, songs and hymns from different countries. All ages and people with disabilities were accommodated.

15.6   Praying with the World Church

- An image of Christ, with a prayer, from a particular country can be placed next to a candle stand in a church or cathedral together with a prayer from that place. These can be changed weekly, fortnightly or monthly.

- As part of worship in a workshop, or as the focus for a prayer group, a large map of the world can be placed on a table or on the floor. Images of Christ from different countries are placed round the map.

- During the time of prayer, people take turns in placing small night-lights on a country of concern and praying for a person or the people of that country.

- End with a time of quiet prayer and reflection as you look at the candles covering the map or use printed prayers from different countries in a closing act of worship. Resource material will be needed.

16.   Healing and reconciliation

The way the images are used will depend on the purpose of the exercise. But it is far less threatening to use a picture in talking through a difficulty than having a face-to-face discussion, whether this be about relationships or illness, bereavement or suffering, anxiety or anger, fears or painful memories, personal hurts or traumas. Working with images is likely to be an emotional experience and must be handled with care.

16.1   A healing exercise using images

- People can take part in a healing exercise on their own with a counsellor or spiritual director, or in a small supportive group.

- Images selected for this exercise are defined by its purpose. One or two pictures may be as effective as a full display, but care must be taken not to pre-judge the situation in choosing the pictures. Generally a wide selection is advisable, including symbolic representations of Christ.

- Depending on the purpose of the exercise, invite the person to choose an image which connects with his or her situation or present feelings. Allow sufficient time for meditation before moving into a time of sharing.

- If a minister is present, such an exercise could be followed by confession and absolution, a significant part of the healing process. Anointing and laying on of hands with prayer can also be included, by a minister or trained lay people.

16.2   Using images in reconciliation

- Some of the images have reconciliation as their theme as in the banner, entitled 'Be Reconciled to God' in Pietermaritzburg Cathedral, South Africa. It was made during a time of strife in the 'killing fields' of KwaZulu-Natal and shows a torn cross, patched together, with images of violence and protest in the background.

- Such images can be used for discussion or quiet reflection and prayer, followed by a suitable act of worship. Mission societies provide appropriate resource material.

- This exercise would be useful in a group experiencing conflict using the images to raise and explore the relevant issues, before moving on to a liturgical act of reconciliation.

17.   Worship

17.1   Using images of Christ in worship

- Following on from any of the exercises, display the combined images of the group or small groups in the middle of the worship space before the altar or Lord's table. They can be placed in the form of a cross, a circle or any other appropriate arrangement as a focus for meditation, prayer, healing, reconciliation, celebration and thanksgiving.

- Worship can take the form of a set liturgical service such as morning prayer, evening prayer, compline or the Eucharist, or it can be an informal time for prayer, meditation and praise.

- When working with images from around the world, it is helpful to have liturgical material that reflects their diversity. USPG, CAFOD and Christian Aid provide worship booklets for different seasons and with different themes such as poverty, medical concerns, debt relief, refugees, AIDS, etc.

- If participants are unsure about singing hymns and songs in other languages, or to unfamiliar tunes, recorded music is helpful in giving them confidence and providing a musical backing.

- Ideally, participants are given a free rein in decorating the worship area, moving the furniture round if necessary, and composing their own liturgy, to make it truly 'the work of the people'. A co-ordinating group is helpful to ensure that everybody knows what they are doing and that the worship flows seamlessly together.

- Resource material should be made available such as a Bible, a cross or crucifix, a range of prayer manuals, printed liturgies (for all seasons, the liturgical year, and from different countries), images to project on a screen, a world map, candles, symbolic objects, incense, drapery and small baskets with blank notelets and pencils for prayers. Flowers, branches, stones, water, shells, etc. can be collected in the surrounding area and used decoratively.

- Appropriate music, recorded or live, chanting, drama, liturgical or circle dancing can all be used to enhance the worship experience.

17.2 Stations of the Cross

Stations of the Cross are usually present on the walls of churches of a more Catholic persuasion; but a set of Stations from Latin America or Africa could enrich one's devotions, especially on Good Friday. A range of worldwide liturgical material with suitable readings and prayers is available. The Benedictine nuns of Turvey Abbey have also produced a colourful modern set of Stations.

17.3 Movement and mysticism: The hymn of Jesus from the Acts of John

This ancient hymn may date from as early as 130 AD and is believed to be a mystery ritual, possibly the earliest traceable Christian ritual. It could be used as a circle dance following work with images.[19]

5

Enlarging our Vision of Christ

Images that challenge and surprise

It is easy to fall into the trap of thinking that religious art would by its very nature have a profound spiritual impact. We are warned, however, that in reality, religious images can close down discussion and exploration because they confirm our stereotypes and preconceptions. Work that challenges and surprises is far more likely to have a powerful spiritual impact.[1] This has indeed been our experience with many of the images of Christ, and may also shed light on the widespread popularity of exhibitions of religious art, which marked the millennium celebrations in Britain.

In many parts of the country, in churches, cathedrals and art galleries people flocked in record-breaking numbers to be surprised and challenged by images of 'How we see Jesus'. And this interest has been sustained. The travelling exhibition of the Methodist Church Collection of Modern Christian Art is but one example.[2] Cathedrals have also played their part in acquiring contemporary works of art and mounting exhibitions. Contrast such enthusiasm with the steady decline in formal religious practice and one has some idea of the spiritual hunger that is waiting to be assuaged through visual imagery, symbol and myth.

During 2001, the millennial exhibition on *Seeing Salvation* at the National Gallery in London attracted thousands of people. Many more watched the accompanying documentary series on television. Neil McGregor, former director of the National Gallery, believes that the enduring fascination for many people is in seeing how artists have grappled with the paradoxes of faith that have shaped western European culture over the centuries: 'From early Christians in the Roman catacombs to Salvador Dali, [they] have tackled the problem of showing Christ as both human and divine, as both victim and conqueror: one man, but the whole of humanity.'[3]

McGregor reminds us that as Jews, Jesus and his followers 'would have recoiled from the idea of an image of the divine under any circumstance'.[4] Nor were the first Christians concerned about how Jesus looked. What mattered to them was what he did – as their Saviour. It is only later, as the Church's devotion became more focused on the person of Jesus, that the need arose for visual images of Christ. McGregor agrees that, even though the gospel texts leave us free to imagine how Jesus looked, artists representing him over the centuries have had to decide on a particular image that is, 'unavoidably, a theology'. Furthermore, by universalizing the particular events in the life of Christ the artist is able to relate the great themes of creation, motherhood, birth, suffering, death, bereavement and separation to our human experience. This archetypal imagery is what touches people so deeply. But in each generation the problem remains of how to depict Christ so that he becomes a living reality.[5] McGregor's concern is with European religious images, but these same issues are just as pertinent in other cultures and contexts.

In our present day, ignorance of the Christian tradition is a quite different sort of challenge. The *Images of Salvation* project, carried out jointly by St John's College, Nottingham, and the University of York, has proved its worth in introducing the Bible to undergraduates in English literature, who were struggling to make sense of their studies. Using the latest technology, the riches of medieval art, whether they are illuminated manuscripts, stained glass or sculptures, have been made available on a CD-ROM, with explanatory notes. This has proved equally useful in other disciplines as well as in schools and churches of all denominations. Because most people now learn visually, this presentation is easily accessible and leaves people free to respond without feeling coerced. Dee Dyass, the director of the project, compares the use of a contemporary visual aid with the way clergy in the Middle Ages used paintings to communicate the Christian faith to a largely illiterate population.[6]

An unashamedly public use of imagery is the large, round icon, 'Christ in Community', affixed to an outer wall of St George's Church in Tufnell Park, north London. Painted by four members of the congregation in 1998, the icon is an outstanding example of how a church can give visible expression to its vision of mission – that the Christian faith is found and lived in community – both to its own congregation and the world outside. The central image of Christ expresses his compassion and love, with a dove above symbolizing the Spirit of God. Christ is surrounded by smaller figures: children listening to a story, representing inclusiveness; a naked woman of sorrows, speaking of a place where it is safe to be vulnerable and sad; a saxophone player, symbolizing celebration and love of music; and a kneeling figure with masks, reflecting the different moods of living and the drama in our lives. The words 'dreams and nightmares', 'hopes and fears' and 'Christ in community', represent the ethos of St George's in trying to contain all shades of life, encircled by a golden thread of love.

The popularity of this icon in workshops signifies the power of visual imagery to communicate meaning. This has particular application in the field of advertising. However, the use of Christian iconography does not necessarily equal Christian intent. What is puzzling, therefore, is why experts in communication see potential in using Christian iconography in advertising in an overwhelmingly secular context. If the role of advertising is to add value to a product by investing it with meaning, then why is it thought worthwhile to spend vast sums of money in drawing on Christian imagery? What is the potential that has been identified? This goes far beyond exploiting a pervasive spirituality. What might this say to our understanding, not only of how Christians see Christ, but of how unbelievers do? This would be a fruitful avenue to explore in terms of mission.[7]

Shock tactics seem to be a significant element in trying to grab the public's attention, assuming that consumers will be sufficiently informed to be suitably shocked, or else enjoy a good joke at the Church's expense. I have a collection of commercial advertisements with Jesus being co-opted into promoting anything from cool drinks, beer, wine, music, paper, car repairs and ethical treatment of animals ('Jesus was a Vegetarian', with an orange slice for a halo), to women's clothing, jeans and fashion jewellery. One which raised a furore was a photo of Raquel Welch in a leather bikini, strapped to a cross. Another was the magazine cover headlined 'The Resurrection of David Beckham', the footballer being photographed with arms outstretched and festooned with crucifixes and rosary beads.

Christmas advertisements have used humour as a selling point, such as the Heineken poster showing a nativity scene with Joseph coming out of the stable shouting: 'It's a girl!'; the Tango advert which had two kneeling children praying to the Lord for the soft drink; and the M&S poster of a spread of party fare with the slogan, '12 days just aren't enough at CHRISTM&S'. A newly launched paper company based all its slogans on the nativity: 'It's a sign … Behold! The King of paper is born', 'Jesus he loves me' and 'Behold the chosen one'. The poster campaign of a Bulgarian wine linked its modest start with Jesus' lowly beginnings, claiming: 'Jesus Was Born in a Trough'. Its stated aim was 'to make us forget our preconceptions and judge on merit rather than origin', encouraging us to examine any knee-jerk reaction with a more considered approach.

On a different note, there is the Audi advertisement with a car flanked by two candles on an altar, and the caption: 'Worship here'. And the *Sunday Times* magazine cover, with the message: 'This Sunday Read the Bible. *Style*, the new bible of fashion and fitness. Worship it, every Sunday'. One might well ask, 'What is going on here?' Nowadays, secular imagery has supposedly supplanted the historical dominance of religious imagery. Why, then, does the advertising industry invest so much in Christian iconography? Do they purposefully risk antagonizing a small minority or are the numbers of complainants deemed too insignificant to count? The latter must have some power as the Heineken advert was withdrawn. Such questions can be explored further in exercises below.

In complete contrast, national Church advertising has tried to reverse the symbolic exchange by co-opting the power of popular images, symbols and language in its effort to shed fusty religious connotations and communicate a more contemporary message. Their unambiguous purpose is to reach 'the unreached', or those on the fringe of the Church. This has not always been appreciated among some Christians, bent on defending the status quo. The marketing drive of the National Alpha Initiative has been the most visible. Designed to attract newcomers, especially young singles, by making the Church seem accessible and fun, its poster billboards and leaflet campaigns focus on the packaging of Christianity in an Alpha course. A typical example: 'Dome. Bug. Party. Alka-Seltzer. Is there more to the Millennium? An opportunity to explore the meaning of life, with Alpha'.

In a drive to fill churches at Christmas and Easter, the Church's Advertising Network has repeatedly landed itself in controversy with its provocative copy. It started cautiously in 1991 with, 'Give Jesus a birthday present – wrap up the kids and take them to church'. But the 1998 poster with its Che Guevara 'Jesus as revolutionary hero' picture caused much controversy, as did the trendy imagery and wording of a poster proclaiming: 'Bad Hair Day?! You're a virgin, you've just given birth, and now three kings have shown up. Make room for God this Christmas'. This had the original idea of reworking Christ's usage of parable in relation to people's experience, in a contemporary form. In contrast, the usual church advertising was said to be more likely 'hand-written in felt-tip pen, flapping desperately in the wind behind cling-film or in a freezer bag'.[8]

How many churches do in fact give serious thought to what and how they communicate? Who are they trying to reach and with what vision of mission, as exemplified by St George's, Tufnell Park? Many don't even have the correct service times displayed on their notice boards, as I know to my cost.

In the United States, the Episcopal Church used a soft-sell approach in its television adverts, showing a wilted daisy reviving, a snuffed-out candle relighting and cuddly puppies feeding from their mother, while the New Church Episcopal Centre in Maryland was more hard-edged in its campaign, using a historic crucifixion scene with the words, 'Of course people with pierced body parts are welcome in our church' scratched over it. Birmingham Diocese caused an uproar in following suit with 'Body Piercing? Jesus had this done 2,000 years ago'. A critical analysis of what the churches were trying to achieve in their different approaches could provide an imaginative new way of thinking about the visual role of contextual theology in mission.

In a workshop, some images of Christ may well offend. Reasons given range from their being too sentimental, trivial or distasteful; to liberties being taken in following popular traditions and romanticizing the gospel story; to their being downright heretical. Even so, such iconography can provoke profound theological discussion and raise ethical issues which otherwise might not have been addressed. Cooper suggests that if the purpose of images is simply to enable discussion of theological ideas that already exist, then the quality of art doesn't matter. However, if we are looking to art and artists to enable both new ways of experiencing and encountering God, and new ways of thinking about God, then the art has to be correspondingly deep. Both 'good' artists and 'good' poets 'go intuitively beyond the horizon that presents a barrier to intellectual reasoning, blazing a trail for the thinkers, who catch up later'.[9] Again, this applies as much to images of Christ from the south as to the more familiar north.

Discovering the multicultural richness of Christ

We have already discussed the legacy of racism and cultural imperialism in implanting foreign norms, values and beliefs in non-western cultures; and of how, in the re-imaging of Christ from an indigenous perspective, artists around the world have sought to liberate themselves and their contemporaries from such shackles. As we seek to interpret what they are saying about how they see Jesus, they are able to unlock us from our culturally biased stereotypes, and give us new eyes to see the incarnate God acting, interacting, healing and suffering in situations quite different from our own.

In some instances the indigenous artists respond to theological ideas merely by illustrating them from within their own cultures: dressing Christ up in Asian, African or Latin American clothes and setting the gospel stories in their local context. In others they are actually engaged in doing theology, witnessing to 'the unity in diversity that is the Trinity', and allowing us to enter into the visual expression of their Christian faith at a far greater depth. At whatever level, the diversity of this imagery will surely enlarge our vision in discovering the full richness of Christ, and may even assist us in overcoming racial and cultural divides.[10]

A good example is the story of Andrew Atagotaaluk, an Inuit (Eskimo) soapstone carver and hunter's son from Pond Inlet in the Northwest Territories of Canada. As a child, he led a nomadic life living off the land, hunting and fishing, building igloos and sod houses, and speaking in his native tongue, Inuktitut. But the assimilation policy of the Canadian government decreed that he be sent away to an English-speaking residential school for an extended period of time so as to be absorbed into the dominant western culture. Unlike his older brother, who returned home with an interpreter in order to communicate with his family, Atagotaaluk retained his home language. He was well placed, therefore, to serve as translator at an evangelistic mission in the high Arctic. He had been baptized in the Anglican Church but, until this time, Jesus was only a Bible story. During the mission, Jesus became a real person in Atagotaaluk's life and he went on to receive theological training and be ordained.

Atagotaaluk's faith was transformed again when he came to realize that although God had called him as an Inuit person, he was presenting Christ from a white perspective. He now saw the need to see Jesus as an Inuit, and to do things the way Jesus did, but in an Inuit way. As he says: 'It's essential for you to be who you are, in your own culture and language, and God loves and respects you for this'.[11] He compares his faith in an Inuit Christ to the way a soapstone carver creates his works of art:

> If you were to see the stone before the carver touched it and gave it the life that it has, you would not be impressed. It is only a rough piece of stone, a chunk of unshaped rock. It is the carver who gives it the life it has ... I believe that when you have faith in Christ, you are shaped by Christ to become what you really are inside yourself – just as the rock is shaped by the vision of the carver. The carver sees beyond the rough outer rock to the possibilities of the beauty of the carving. He shapes it to be what he sees within the rock ... This is how it is with life in Christ. Each person becomes more what he/she really is in their own culture.[12]

In his concern for the loss of identity among his people, and the concomitant social breakdown, Atagotaaluk believes that they must remain true to their heritage even as they are shaped by Christ. Contrary to government policy, they must become more of what they are, and not set their traditions aside to take on someone else's way of life. 'Christ is the fulfilment of our own culture,' he says, 'our own language and our own understanding of life. When we are in Christ, and we follow Christ, there is a beauty in the image of who we are just as there is beauty in the carvings which are carved in the vision of the carver'.[13] It was precisely because of his efforts to restore his people's pride – helping them to take responsibility for their lives, find their own solutions to their problems and recover their traditional knowledge – that Atagotaaluk was elected the first Anglican bishop of the high Arctic.

Similarly, Richard West reaches out to us in an image of a Native American Christ in a rock-strewn Garden of Gethsemane. The agony of this kneeling figure, with his working man's hands gripped tautly together, eyes uplifted and lips parted in prayer, becomes *our* agony, *our* moment of truth. On another level, the Gethsemane experience resonates with the Vision Quest of Native American people, as does Jesus' time in the wilderness. In this rite of passage, a young man goes to a high place to be alone with God and seek an understanding of his own true self. Through fasting and prayer, meditation and repentance, he grapples with the dark forces of his interior soul while he waits on the Great Spirit to give him a vision of what is expected of him in this life. West crosses cultural boundaries to confront us with the same questions, and indeed it is an image with which many people have identified.

In the Apache Christ, Jesus is depicted as a Mescalero holy man from New Mexico standing atop the Sierra Blanca, the sacred mountain of the Apaches. He is greeting the sun on the fourth morning of the women's puberty rites, the most sacrosanct of Apache ceremonies, celebrating the sanctity of the gift of producing new life. The painting is subtitled 'Giver of Life', an Apache name for God, and is redolent with symbols associated with traditional rites such as a deer rattle, eagle feather, grass brush and bags of tobacco, together with Greek letters depicting Christ's name. As we start to unpack the many layers of meaning in the icon, the unknown artist breaks open the theological discourse on new life in Christ, and challenges us to be 'surprised by God'.

Crossing continents to Africa, there has been a concerted move among black people to integrate African cosmology with their contemporary experience of life. As the South African theologian, Tinyiko Maluleke, so cogently notes, 'Africans are doing a lot of things to Jesus. They are making him sing and dance. They speak through him and he through them.' For Maluleke, Jesus is no longer the high and mighty king, far removed from the world below, nor is he obsessed with judging sinners. Rather, he is a healer without equal, who 'makes people to "be all right" ', and enables them to deal with the realities of their lives:

> He is a screaming Jesus – screaming on the cross and screaming in Africa, on the pulpits, in the streets and in the squatter camp. The African Christ who smiles on the cross is a paradox inviting reflection. This is a defiant smile. A smile that smiles away the pain of the cross. Africans are taking Jesus by the hand, teaching him a few African 'moves'

and sensitising him to local issues and conditions.[14]

New faces of the African Christ depict him as a chief, traditional doctor, story-teller, ancestor, elder brother, master of initiation, folk hero, the black Messiah, sacrificial offering, foot-washer of the unlovely, friend of the poor and the oppressed, resident of informal settlements, lover of sinners, milk basket of heaven, the great blanket (offering protection), hunter of souls, and much more.

Jackson Hlungwani is a black South African who has sought to express radical new christological imagery in his art. An ordained minister in the African Zionist Church, he became founder-leader of his own group, Jerusalem One Christ, in Gazankulu. He claims that his stone and wood sculptures, symbolic and apocalyptic rather than narrative in their imagery, are divinely inspired by the Trinity, the artist being but a channel to communicate God's image. In his mopani wood sculpture of *Christ the Soccer Champion* (1993, Sasol Art Museum, Stellenbosch), Jesus is revealed as a popular hero of urban African culture. But this soccer star, with leg extended in the act of scoring a goal, does not celebrate his triumph with extravagant gestures. Nor do the heavy, knotted limbs carved out of a forked tree trunk present him as a Beckham-like icon of grace and beauty. Rather, with one lumpy hand pressed against his ear, this crude image depicts Christ as an empathetic listener intent on hearing the sighs and groans of the people above the roars of the football fans.[15]

Fr Frans Claerhout, a Belgian missionary, is one of the few white artists who have attempted to contextualize Jesus in South Africa. He has long incarnated a black Christ in the Orange Free State milieu of his Roman Catholic mission. Christ is born anew in fields of sunflowers and corn, or else in the shanty dwellings of local informal settlements.[16] While Claerhout's colourful pictures may seem to romanticize harsh realities, during the apartheid era, the thought that Jesus might be born as a poor black man in a squatter camp was a radical take on theology.

Art works exhibited in St George's Cathedral, Cape Town in 1994 of *Jesus suffering from AIDS* were more controversial. This display caused a furore. People were slow to comprehend what the dramatic representation of the compassion and suffering of Christ might mean to those stigmatized and excluded by disease, black and white alike.

A photograph taken during the liberation struggle in the 1980s offers a different challenge. It shows a shattered crucifix lying face down on the floor, arms broken, in St Joseph's Catholic Church in Phokeng, near Rustenburg. The result of a bomb blast, it was almost certainly caused by government forces. The shocking part is that the perpetrators would have been ardent churchgoers, used to family prayers and daily Bible-reading. When the structures of society are pervaded by sin, Christianity demands a lot more than just filling the pews, paying your dues and singing 'Alleluia'.

In working with images we are also encouraged to dialogue with other faiths for the story of Christ has inspired many non-Christian artists. K.C.S. Paniker, a leading Indian painter, is a liberal Hindu, but in studying the Bible he was moved by the sacrificial offering of Jesus for love. His paintings and sculptures have included *Woman Taken in Adultery*, *Blessed are the Peace-Makers*, *Healing of the Leper* and *Sorrow of Christ*.[17] Marc Chagall provides another example of inter-faith Christology. Son of Russian Hassidic Jews, he too was touched by the suffering of Christ as shown in his paintings of the crucifixion. He invariably expressed his Jewish roots with Old Testament imagery; but in his *White Crucifixion*, he actually depicts Jesus as a Jew, prayer shawl and all, suffering on the cross among persecuted Jewish people. However, it is in the breaking down of gender barriers that we have the most radical expressions in the re-imaging of Christ.

Women re-imaging Christ

In the image of Jesa Christa, a feminine depiction of Christ, both men and women artists use christological symbols to explore the specific suffering of women, or their nurturing role as mother. So, for example, in his *Resurrection, Cookham*, Stanley Spencer depicts Christ in a maternal role cradling babies in his arms. As a man, and considering that this was well before the feminist movement, his re-imaging of Christ as a female figure shows great depth and insight. So, too, women's images of a male Christ have their own authenticity, coming as they do from a womanist theological perspective. As yet another way of enlarging our vision of Christ, we now look at how women from different cultures have retold the story of Jesus through their art.

Over the centuries women worldwide have experienced the threefold oppression of racism, sexism and poverty as much in the Church as in wider society. Those who suffered most under the yoke of power, privilege and class were the poorest of the poor, the majority being female and black. The African American theologian, Jacqueline Grant, suggests that the central christological problem arising out of the triple bondage of women 'rests in the fact that Jesus Christ historically has been and remains imprisoned by the socio-political interests of those who have historically been the keepers of principalities and powers. This Jesus has been a primary tool for undergirding oppressive structures'.[18]

No matter their colour or condition, since the beginning of Christendom women everywhere have suffered exclusion within a patriarchal Church. Feminine models of spirituality recorded in the Scriptures have long been systematically ignored, as in Isaiah (42.14; 46.3; 49.15; 66.9), and in the biblical accounts of Jesus' mutually enriching encounters with women (cf. Matthew 9.18-26; Mark 12.41-44, 16.1-8; Luke 8.1-3, 10.38-42, 13.10-13, 15.8-10, 18.1-8; John 4.1-41, 8.1-11, 11.1-44, etc.). Throughout history, these have been passed over as incidental while the exclusively male oligarchy had no qualms in pressing into service the Pauline strictures derogatory to

women in order to sustain their marginalization in the Church.

Male domination and control have been reinforced through religious imagery which emphasizes the maleness of Jesus and his disciples. I remember a workshop with diocesan missioners and evangelists in which we reflected on pictures of *The Last Supper* within the context of an extended Eucharist. Two Anglican women deacons from Wales, where the ordination of women was much delayed, were heartbroken by the overwhelming masculinity of the images. The men were somewhat surprised and embarrassed by their emotional reaction, which well illustrates the ambiguity of working with images. Reading them is a very subjective matter. We can all see the things we want to see and ignore or reject any aspects we wish to avoid.[19] But in exploring how women artists themselves have created images of Christ, we approach the subject from a quite different perspective and this can be profoundly moving, and challenging, to both sexes.

Most women still find the status quo hard to confront, the more so as their suppression has been sanctified by centuries of indoctrination which has imparted religious significance to their subordination. Men still remain entrenched as authority figures in the higher echelons of the Church whether this is in worship, ecclesiastical roles, or Church structures, while women find approval by staying submissive, docile and dependent. As Doris Jean Dyke wryly remarks, 'Since theology is always contextual, these values are clearly established in Christian doctrine'.[20] It is only comparatively recently that women around the world have made the radical move of discarding traditional images of Jesus which perpetuated their oppression, and discovered him anew for themselves. In so doing they found freedom and self-respect in coming to a fresh understanding of their worth as well as their faith.

Oppressed people themselves, especially women, have long taken the initiative in challenging the dominant status quo in song, as in the African-American spirituals. Carefully coded language masked their true intent as freedom songs from slavery. Religious art is a much more recent outlet for black women in Northern America in exposing and confronting their oppression. This is exemplified in the paintings of Coral Bernadine, which hang in St Michael's Roman Catholic Church, Black Rock Cultural Centre, Barbados.

In her dramatic portrayal of the *Survivors of the Middle Passage* (1992), Bernadine celebrated the 'discovery' of the West Indies by Christopher Columbus 500 years earlier by exalting those who had resisted colonial oppression. Centre stage is a slave owner on horseback wielding a whip. To his left are half-naked African men, women and children in chains against a backdrop of stormy seas symbolizing the horrors of their journey from West Africa. To his right are slaves triumphantly breaking their chains together with gun-toting women. Heroes of the freedom movement, such as Marcus Garvey, Martin Luther King, Bob Marley and Harriet Tubman, feature prominently. This powerful testimony to a black womanist consciousness permeates all Bernadine's religious art.

In *The Crucifixion*, a dark-skinned Jesus is surrounded by cameos of him comforting the poor, cleansing the temple and rising in glory. At the foot of the cross is Bernadine's trademark, the Isaiahan image of a lion lying down with a lamb. Three other lions in the picture may well symbolize a more aggressive Rastafarian Christology. The Rastafarian Black Messiah, Haile Selassi, was also known as the Lion of Judah, a title of Christ.

Bernadine's portrayal of Mary as *Mother of the Oppressed* (early 1990s) has Jesus as a curly-haired, bare-chested, brown youth gazing up at a matronly Caribbean Mary enthroned in heavenly splendour. With stigmata clearly visible on his palms, the resurrected Jesus grasps the hand of a naked, skeletal figure, showing his compassion for, and identification with, the suffering of black people. In the many faces filling the rest of the picture, Tubman, Garvey and King appear together with Nelson Mandela and Haile Selassi. The Pope is the only white face, reflecting Bernadine's commitment to her Catholic faith.

Many of the revolutionary Nicaraguan artists, in *The Gospel in Art by the Peasants of Solentiname*,[21] are also women. In their brightly coloured, 'primitive' paintings, their faith in 'the living word of the living God' is incarnated in the ordinary, everyday life of their island home on Lake Nicaragua. Jesus is portrayed as a poor, bearded *campesino* like them. His story comes alive in being depicted within the dramatic events of these people's struggle for liberation, and the horrors of the ravaging of Solentiname by Somoza's National Guard in 1977. The imaginative way in which biblical scenes take flesh in the Nicaraguan context is a powerful testimony to the enduring hope of these people in the good news of the kingdom, even under persecution.

Moving on to Africa, Teresa Hinga, a feminist theologian from Kenya, argues that even though the colonial Christ came as Conqueror, Africans made him their own through an independent reading of the Bible. Hinga offers three indigenous concepts of Christ which impact on African women. Most popular is Christ as personal saviour and friend because these women need a comforter to help them bear their pain and suffering. Jesus as embodiment of the Holy Spirit comes next. He is 'the voice of the voiceless, the power of the powerless' for women at the bottom of the pile, who find solace in the charismatic African Initiated Churches. Finally, there is the prophetic Jesus who challenges the socio-economic injustices of the status quo.[22]

For the majority of African women, a liberative Christology is usually expressed orally through prayer, preaching, songs and hymns. Religious art has been sadly neglected, the Roman Catholic Church being the exception, though here it is still in embryonic form. In Southern Africa, woven and embroidered tapestries are the preferred medium in imaging Christ, focusing on traditional themes such as the nativity, Madonna and child, Christ's ministry, the Last Supper and the risen Christ. Their most radical innovation is in depicting Christ as black. Patriarchy is still a powerful force in suppressing women's emancipation in Africa.

Not surprisingly, parallels can be drawn between African and Asian women's Christology because of similar experiences of oppression. Asian women have also rejected the received images of Jesus as 'triumphal King' and 'authoritative high priest'; but their re-imaging of Christ has far more bite. According to the Korean feminist theologian, Chung Hyun Kyung, the prevailing image of Jesus as suffering servant reflects most women's experience. However, Filipino women differentiate between the passive suffering imposed by an oppressor, which is their daily lot and comparable to Jesus' story, and an active liberative suffering where Jesus accompanies them in their struggle for justice. Both aspects are significant in giving these women dignity as they carry the cross of Christ every step of the way and undergo his passion in offering up their lives for their people.[23] Such is their identification with the crucified Christ that one will say to another, 'Move over, it is my turn on the cross.'

This Christology resonates with the work of the Chinese artist, Taeko Tomiyama from Manchuria, who became actively involved in liberation struggles after meeting with mine workers during the labour strikes of 1960. She asks:

What is painting? Is it a beautiful flower blooming out of a life of affluence? Is it nothing more than a prized possession which is passively admired for its lines or lovely colours? Or does it provoke some sort of human change in those who behold the painting prompting them to action? Does it create the spark that leads to liberation?[24]

There is no doubting where Tomiyama stands. Her powerful painting of the *Pieta of Kwangju* (*The Christ We Share*, no. 29) was done after the people's occupation of this Korean city was brutally suppressed by military forces. In the *Pieta*, the eternal suffering of women is vividly captured in Mary's grief, with her exaggeratedly large eyes and a single tear coursing down her cheek. Jesus' head is cradled in her lap, his body stretched out before her on the ground. A wailing figure with outstretched arms kneels behind. The agony of the event is intensified by depicting all three figures in black and white against a blood red background.[25]

A common thread runs through all the depictions of Jesus which are emerging from Asian women's movements in countries such as India, Indonesia, Korea, Sri Lanka and the Philippines. Chung Hyun Kyung identifies three clusters of images – Jesus as Liberator, Revolutionary and Political Martyr; Jesus as Mother, Woman and Shaman; and Jesus as Worker. Together they represent 'a Christological transformation created out of Asian women's experiences as they struggle for full humanity'.[26]

In Australia's Northern Territory, painting has generally been the task of aboriginal men. Miriam-Rose Ungunmerr from Daly River Mission, not only broke new ground as a woman in painting a series of Stations of the Cross for her church in 1974, but she used traditional stylistic patterns. These draw on ancient symbols which go beyond external shapes to express inner meanings and emotions. The profound faith which pervades her painting of *The Third Station – Simon of Cyrene Helps Jesus Carry the Cross*, is reflected in her prayer: 'Jesus take up your heavy cross. It gives you pain. Help all who suffer. Forgive us for the pain we give you and others,'[27] (*The Christ We Share*, no. 20). Another Australian, Margaret Ackland, is equally innovative in having women and children join the men round the table in her *Last Supper* (1993). Seated across the table from Christ is a breast-feeding mother, 'serving to amplify and make present the symbols of this meal of nourishment and hope'.[28]

In the contemporary European scene, women artists appear to favour four themes in their re-imaging of Christ: a softer womanist imagery, the nurturing and loving service of a mother, compassion in the presence of suffering, and contextualizing Jesus in everyday experience. There is little evidence of an exploration of political and social issues beyond the gender ones, and the raw emotions reflected in the religious art of Third World women is generally absent.

An example of womanist imagery is the eight-metre-high tapestry of Else Marie

Jakobsen of Norway in which she portrays the triumphant risen Christ with feminine face, hair and hands and flowing robes.[29] The painting of *The Foot Washing* by the English artist, Kathy Priddis, exemplifies the theme of motherly nurturing and love. Here Jesus is depicted as the servant-king, washing the feet of Peter. Their heads are closely joined in an intimate bonding as Peter reaches out to be embraced by Christ (*The Christ We Share*, no. 23).

The power of the suffering love of women is palpable in the bronze *Pieta* (1937/8) by Kathe Kollwitz of Germany. It is found in a small memorial chapel on Unter den Linden not far from the Berlin Wall in the former eastern sector, and commemorates those killed in two world wars. Kollwitz's son died in the trenches in the First World War and in her sculpture the body of Christ is almost lost in the enveloping embrace of his grief-stricken mother.[30]

Lastly, the down-to-earth style of Dinah Roe Kendall's colourful and witty illustrations give new life and meaning to the gospel story as it is re-enacted in multicultural, multiracial Sheffield in the British midlands (2002). Gillian Bell Richards is another whose context-ualization of a very human, contemporary Christ, whether this is in the wilderness, the Garden of Gethsemane or on the road to Emmaus, reflects the present experience of many British people.

Two American women artists have also captured the sheer humanity of Jesus who is present in us all if we care to look. In *Jesus of the People* Janet McKenzie has a haunting image of a youthful African-American Jesus looking directly at us, flanked by indigenous symbols including a feather which represents the Great Spirit of the Native American people. Although this Jesus is a man, McKenzie used a woman model to embody the feminine aspect.[31] In contrast, Marylyn Felion's watercolour of *Christ as Poor, Black, Death Row Inmate* is all male. The portrait is of a prisoner, 'the most God-filled person' whom Felion ever knew, and who she accompanied to the electric chair in Nebraska in 1997. His serene smile at his death reflected his sure knowledge that he had been forgiven for the wrongs he had done and that he was going home to the Lord.[32]

However, some of the most powerful statements by women artists in the West have been their re-imaging of Christ as a crucified woman, with or without the cross and usually naked. These often contro-versial images raise a host of questions about how we relate to our bodies and how women find healing in identifying with the passion of Christ.

Jesa Christa crucified

The theological concept of Jesa Christa crucified is about female figures taking on the kenotic or self-emptying persona of Jesus. Dame Holy Wisdom (*Hagia Sophia*) in the Book of Proverbs is the Old Testament female icon prefiguring Jesus with whom she shares many salient traits. She is a divine person present at the beginning of creation (3.19; 8.22-23). She invites humanity 'to eat of my bread and drink of my wine' (9.5). Though divine, she comes down into the market place and cries out aloud in the streets (1.20-21; 8.2-3). Like Christ, she suffers rejection and scoffing (1.22-30). Some other notable kenotic female figures in Christian history include Hagar, the pregnant bondswoman cast out by a jealous Sarah (Genesis 16), Mary the mother of Jesus, and the other three Marys who stood alongside her at the foot of the cross, sharing in the holy suffering of Jesus.

One may see the figure of Jesa Christa as a theological statement about the pristine nature of Christ transcending and embracing both male and female forms. The masculinity of Jesus is not an inalienable part of his humanity. God did not become a man *per se*. He became human. Women extend Jesus' humanity to include femininity. One of the contentions against the ordination of women to the priesthood was that only men were considered to be potential icons of Christ, sharing Christ's manhood. But the womanist understanding of Christology interprets God becoming human, both male and female.

Jesa Christa crucified can also be seen as the radical revelation of the suffering of women which is not passive, but redemptive and transformative. In that sense Jesa Christa is more than a political re-imaging of a male Jesus evoking pity and outrage. It is a sacred image of transcendence relevant to the spirituality of both sexes although, as an icon, it exclusively tells the story of women and feminine categories such as motherland and earth, using numinous christological imagery.

The earliest such image in my collection is of a twelfth-century fresco of *The Female in the Godhead*, in Orschalling. It depicts a female figure, probably the Holy Spirit, supported by two bearded male figures, one young and one old, presumably Jesus and God. Investing a woman with divinity is already making a statement about the divine becoming vulnerable. There does not have to be a cross. Even where a cross is present it can be a male fantasy about bondage rather than suffering as in *The Temptation of St Anthony* by Felicien Rops, 1878. Symbolic of the temptations that St Anthony (286-306), the first Desert Father, underwent in order to explore his vocation, a voluptuous, naked, female figure, though tied to a wooden cross, is smiling and has her hair wreathed in flowers. Freud cited this work as a metaphor for 'the typical case of repression', but Rops' work was well before Freud and created an outcry in the pious atmosphere of his native Belgium.[33]

Over a hundred years later, the American artist, James Murphy, sculpted a two-foot figure of a woman, hands and feet nailed to a cross, which unapologetically represents a female crucifixion. Entitled *Christine on the Cross*, it was exhibited in St James Chapel at Union Theological Seminary in New York in 1984. Murphy was inspired by his realization 'that the world's rejection and hatred of women culminates in crucifying the female Christ'.[34] However, in the last three decades women themselves have set their own imprint on the imaging of Jesa Christa crucified, with newly won perspectives feeding in to their contextualization of theology through art.

In 1974, Edwina Sandys, American artist and granddaughter of Winston Churchill, sculpted her *Christa* for the United Nations Decade for Women. The bronze figure is of a nude female, with head drooping and arms outstretched on a cross. Sandys sees her *Christa* as representing 'the oppressed and devoured women of our jails and prisons, any woman forgotten, hidden, abused or thrown away, the suffering of women in all of us' (*The Christ We Share*, no. 30). The sculpture was exhibited in the Episcopal Cathedral of St John the Divine, New York, in 1984 with the intention of opening people's 'eyes and hearts to the presence of the feminine in the Judeo-Christian tradition and show[ing] the power and the vulnerability of the Christ within each of us'. Some thought *Christa* 'a desecration' but for the Dean it achieved its purpose in forcing people to think theologically and to be confronted by their bondage to stereotypes and literalness.

A similar though larger sculpture, *Crucified Woman*, by the Canadian artist Almuth Lutkenhaus-Lackey, was even more controversial. None the less, this striking seven-foot bronze has empowered many people, especially women, to reflect on their faith and talk about it in their own words, often for the first time. Made in 1976, the elongated female figure is in cruciform shape, naked, with outstretched arms. There is no cross and no nail marks.

Dyke makes the point that a woman does not have to hang on a cross, because for many their lives are a perpetual crucifixion. The ballet-like pose evokes a resurrection theme, comparable with the image of a dancing risen Christ found in Asian Christology. The beauty of the erect, youthful body with its taut breasts is in painful contrast to the sorrowing, scored face, head inclined to one side.

Crucified Woman was first hung in the chancel of Bloor Street United Church in Toronto, over Easter 1979, causing a major outcry. Seven years later controversy followed it to its permanent home in the garden of Emmanuel College, a United Church theological college in the University of Toronto. The bronze has been vilified by some as heretical, obscene, blasphemous and even erotic. But many people have been forced to grapple with issues that are at the heart of women's theology, and be transformed in the process. This includes Christ being seen to represent all humanity, not just men, and the need for people to be shaken free from their patriarchal theology in order to experience afresh the redemptive message and power of the cross.

According to Dyke, many women, including those from other faith traditions, have been able to identify their own sufferings and struggles with the strength, anguish, beauty, pain and suffering of *Crucified Woman*, and so experience healing and wholeness.[35] Another such sculpture entitled *INRI* by Bettina Rheims in France (c. 1998), is also without a cross but has the more typical drooping head with crown of thorns, and nails through hands and feet.

In her photograph of *Yo Mama's Last Supper*, hanging in New York's Brooklyn Museum, Renee Cox depicts Christ as a beautiful, nude woman, standing full-frontal behind a table set with a goblet, jug of wine and bowl of fruit. With a long white cloth draped over her outstretched arms, she invites us to the Passover Feast, prefiguring Christ's crucifixion. Similarly, Sam Taylor Wood's photographic represen-tation of Leonardo Da Vinci's *Last Supper*, entitled *Wrecked* (1996), has a bare-breasted woman replacing the figure of Christ.[36]

Shockingly different is *Bosnian Christa* created by the British artist, Margaret Argyle, in mixed textiles during Passiontide, 1993. Here, the image of a woman's open vulva, all in red, frames the slender, nude figure of a crucified woman standing before a cross. The woman is in profile so as not to expose her genitalia. The imagery of a bleeding vulva, symbol-izing the rape of Muslim women during the Bosnian War, is a horrifying reminder of men's inhumanity to women, with the cross transformed as a symbol of suffering for people of all races and all religions.

Other female figures can also take on the persona of Jesus as in the maquette for St Helena, commissioned for the Millennium from Philip Jackson to grace St Helen's Square in the city of York. It shows a young St Helena in cruciform position, holding up a broken cross bar, her head facing down and her feet set on a skull and pile of bones. As the mother of Constantine, St Helena reputedly discovered the true cross of Christ, bringing it back to Europe. Although the story is apocryphal, it represents an external symbol of the inner discovery of the cross and all that that means in our lives. St Helena thus becomes an epiphany of Christ crucified.

The only non-Caucasian image of Jesa Christa crucified in my collection is by a man, Ernesto Lozado-Uzuriaga from Peru, hanging in St Luke's Church, Hillmarton Road, London. Called *Wounded Woman*, it is a roughly drawn picture of a cruciform, nude, female figure, *sans* cross, surrounded by Peruvian imagery of animals, huts and vegetation. The figure represents all of Peruvian womanhood in the totality of their suffering for they bear the brunt of every kind of oppression. Through their vulnerability they take on the persona of Christ, reminding us that Christ continues to be crucified in our midst today.

The story of Maria Cristina Gomez, a Baptist primary school teacher from El Salvador, who died for her faith, epitomizes the lot of Latin American women in their struggle for justice. Her crime was to belong to a Base Christian Community, a group who commit themselves through faith to work for good in their community. In April 1989, she was abducted by heavily armed men as she came out of school, and was tortured and killed. A painted wooden cross was commissioned by her friends to celebrate her life and faith. The typically colourful, indigenous style shows her with arms upraised, more in joy than sadness, surrounded by vignettes of her everyday life as mother, schoolmistress, farmer, Sunday School teacher. In her very ordinariness as a Christian peasant she became a threat to the totalitarian regime and in her martydom took on the persona of the kenotic Christ (*The Christ We Share*, no. 3).

As with St Helena, *Bosnian Christa*, and Maria Gomez, Mary, mother of Christ, is another female figure who is symbolically identified with Jesa Christa crucified. No matter whether Coral Bernadine, a devout Catholic, portrays her Caribbean Mary as a young maiden, a middle-aged mother, or a wise elder, she is transformed into a symbol of liberated humanity representing women as the strength of Caribbean society. Significantly, all Bernadine's Mary pictures bear her trademark of a lion lying down with a lamb.

In *The Power and the Glory* (1985), Mary is depicted as a fulsomely breasted, bare-footed mother in faded, tattered clothing. Surrounded by exotic local vegetation, flowers and fruit, with the sea in the far distance, these images signify regeneration in the Caribbean context. With arms outstretched and eyes closed, Mary stands in front of the crucified Christ, the blood from his wounded palms trickling over her large, rough working hands. Christ's eucharistic sacrifice is symbolized by the Bible, glass of wine and broken loaf of home-made bread on a table alongside, while the altar in Bernadine's church stands behind. In identifying with the broken body of Christ, this humble, black Mary is transformed into a priestly figure who has the power to consecrate, sanctify and bless creation, welcoming in the abundance of the kingdom.

Lastly, the use of christological imagery to represent the feminine categories of motherland and earth is well illustrated in *Birhen ng Balintawak – Our Lady Virgin of Balintawak*. This image of the Madonna and Child is an icon of the Philippine Independent Church (*Iglesia Filipina Independiente*), which broke away from Rome in 1902 as part of a nationalist movement against Spain, America and Japan, and became affiliated to the Anglican Communion. The Virgin's gown displays the colours of the Filipino flag, denoting the Mother Country. This was an overt act of defiance, as the American government had banned the flag, the national anthem and all nationalist demonstrations. Santo Niño, the Holy Child, is dressed as a Katapunan guerilla representing the people's struggle. He stands amidst broken images of power and war, his mission being to overcome oppression and exploitation. Other figures symbolize the partnership of the labouring class with nationalistic clergy in their fight for freedom.

In this image, the traditional Catholic icon of Virgin and Child, used by Spanish colonial forces to subjugate and domesticate the Filipinos, has been transformed into a symbol of their hopes and aspirations. Just as the Jews interpreted the Suffering Servant as Israel, so in the Filipino theology of liberation, this imagery is extended to the Philippines.[37] The feminine symbol of the Virgin as Motherland takes on the persona of the suffering Christ of the people.

Obviously, great sensitivity is needed in working with the images of Jesa Christa crucified. Since returning to South Africa I have used this collection with multiracial groups of Anglican clergy. The women felt liberated by the experience but the African men had problems with the depiction of a woman as invested with divinity, more especially a naked female figure on the cross. This was said to conflict with their culture and indeed I have no such images from Africa. It may well say something about patriarchy and a continent-wide resistance to the ordination of women, which is only slowly being overcome.

The images of Jesa Christa crucified were also mixed in with a large display of the Passion of Christ, as part of an interactive Good Friday service in a multicultural, suburban parish in Cape Town. Significantly, a good number of women of all races ferreted these images out and they too found them profoundly liberating; some were overcome with emotion.

❋ ❋ ❋ ❋ ❋

Exercises to enlarge our vision of Christ

18.   Images that surprise, challenge and inform

18.1   Images of salvation in medieval Christian art

The CD-ROM, *Images of Salvation*, offers a choice of 44 biblical themes illustrated with 180 colour images from medieval Christian art. Individual images come with a detailed commentary on key doctrinal and art historical elements. They can be viewed on a screen, printed on to OHP slides or projected using PowerPoint®. In addition to the basic purpose of this resource to inform, the images can be used to discuss various aspects of the gospel presentation:

* What do the images of Christ tell us about the culture and contexts of the medieval artists? How do the images reflect their day and age?

* Project a selection of images and invite people to suggest titles for Christ, e.g. Christ the King, Saviour, the Monk who rules the world (see Exercise 8). What does this tell us about medieval concepts of Christ? How do they differ from contemporary concepts?

* This resource can be used in teaching or discussion to explore themes such as the nativity, passion and resurrection.

* A comparison can be drawn with contemporary European images of these same themes, as well as with images from around the world. What do the images have in common? What are the significant differences? What does this tell us about how Jesus has been seen then, and now?

* Are there any images on the CD-ROM which surprise or challenge? Discuss why this might be so.

18.2   Studying a single painting in depth: e.g. *The Light of the World*

Holman Hunt's *The Light of the World* would be a good choice as so many people have their own copies and the picture is readily available. This exercise would help them to gain a deeper understanding of the picture. Shown at the Royal Academy in London in 1854, the original now hangs in Keble College, Oxford. The second, smaller version (1851-56), is in Manchester City Art Galleries. A life-size replica, which toured the British colonies in 1905-7, is in St Paul's Cathedral, London. Due to failing eyesight, Hunt (1827-1910) had to be helped by the painter, Edward Hughes, to finish it.

* Invite people to find out all they can about Holman Hunt and his picture before the discussion. Libraries and the internet are good resources. For background information see, for example, *The Image of Christ* (catalogue of the *Seeing Salvation* exhibition 2000).[38] Information on the Pre-Raphaelite Brotherhood would be useful in setting the scene in this period in art.

* Holman Hunt came from an evangelical background and was attracted to biblical symbolism. How is this realized in his choice of text for the painting – Revelation 3.20? Other biblical references inspiring him were John 8.12, Psalm 119.105 and Romans 13.12. What do these texts say about Hunt's understanding of Jesus?

* Invite people who have their own copies of the painting to say what it has meant to them. How might it have enriched their faith? Do they have a story to tell of how it came into their possession — handed down in the family, bought for a special reason, given at confirmation or at another significant time in their life, etc.?

* Has anyone seen the original paintings in Oxford, Manchester or London? What did that mean to them?

* After some initial criticism, the painting achieved great popularity due to huge sales of engravings and numerous illegal photographic copies. Why do you think it is still so popular today?

* Allow time for meditating on the picture. This can be followed by discussion: 'What does the image mean to me today?' 'How does the picture challenge my faith, and my way of life?'

* The picture can be used as a focus for worship. The group can design a simple liturgy around the theme of light, with suitable prayers, hymns, songs or choruses, and reflection on the texts given above. Imagery could include lighted candles or a miner's lamp.

18.3 Using Christian iconography in advertisements

In preparing for this exercise, the group needs to spend some time collecting both commercial and church-related advertisements in magazines, newspapers, posters, fliers, photographs of billboards and Christmas decorations etc., in which Christian iconography is used either to sell products, or to attract people to church. Include copies of Alpha publicity and the Church's Advertising Network posters if possible. The very act of inviting people to participate in the search will raise awareness of some of the issues involved. The two sorts of images are best displayed separately. Allow people time to have a good look before starting the discussion.

18.3.1 Ask people to select an image from either one or both sets of advertisements. You can then use the basic exercise to ask: 'Who is Christ for me in this picture?

18.3.2 Focusing on commercial advertisements, ask:

* Why do advertisers invest so much money in using Christian iconography in the commercial world? What is the potential that they have seen?

* What might this say to our understanding, not only of how Christians see Christ, but of how non-believers do?

* How do the advertisements challenge my faith? If I find some offensive, why is that so? Have I tried to delve deeper?

* Why has the advertiser used an image of Christ, or the nativity, in this way, and what can we learn about Christian faith, even though it may not have been intended?

* If the David Beckham image, or a similar one, is available it can be placed alongside a picture of a crucifixion. Discuss: What is being said about these people? Can they carry the weight of what is being put on their shoulders?

18.3.3 Focusing on church advertising, and depending on the nature of the pictures collected, one can ask:

* Do you think this image communicates a more up-to-date message of the Christian faith, and is it likely to attract 'the unreached' or those on the fringe of the Church?

* What do you think the American Episcopal Church and the New Church Episcopal Centre in Maryland, as mentioned in the text, were trying to achieve in their different approaches? Which approach do you think would be most effective? Who might respond, and why?

* Why do you think the Church's Advertising Network posters have created such controversy among British churchgoers? Do you think the posters would attract people to church at Christmas and Easter?

* What do you think of the advertising for Alpha? How effective is it in reaching people in your community?

* How well does your church communicate in inviting people to join them in worship? Who are they trying to reach? How could communications be improved?

19.   Women re-imaging Christ and Jesa Christa crucified

The text suggests numerous ways in which women's re-imaging of Christ can be studied depending on the availability of images. Questions raised for reflection and discussion would be dependent on the nature and interests of a group, and the purpose of the exercise. Some examples are given:

* How can the images challenge sexual stereotypes and raise the consciousness of both men and women?

* How can the images be used to explore feminist or womanist theology?

* What are the gender issues which the images raise, more especially in the Church? How do the images challenge patriarchal theology?

* How do women's images compare in different contexts and cultures? What are the significant similarities and differences in the issues raised? What role does inculturation play?

* What do the images say about the suffering of women everywhere? Can you differentiate between passive suffering and liberative suffering in your context, as do Asian women?

* What images can you find to explore Jesus' encounters with women? Compare the way men and women portray these stories in art.

* Can you empathize with the way women find healing through identifying with feminine images of the passion of Christ. What are the issues raised and how might these be dealt with in your context?

Postscript

In working with images of Christ we travel the globe, visiting people of faith and encountering the incarnate Christ who is liberated from the shackles with which we have bound him. We do not need to be holy or religious to relate to an image. Nor do we need to be highly educated or have theological expertise. We may belong to a church or not. The Christ who comes to us through images is not the Christ of the professional ministry, but the visible Christ with whom we can interact. We become our own theologians and take responsibility for our own journeys of faith. We discover our own Christologies, not in any abstract, intellectual way, but by reaching in to the multidimensional diversity incarnate in the images.

Through the images, we, the people of God, are empowered to explore our relationship with the mystery of Christ, individually as well as collectively. The focus of our meditation and reflection is not the Jesus of history or eternity, but the Jesus of the here and now, who is forever touching and transforming our lives. This ever newly incarnating Jesus, endowed with many faces, comes to us as the Saviour who offers inexhaustible future possibilities. He affirms every context, allowing peoples of the world to meet him in their unique stories. He is the Jesus of as many Christologies as there are contexts.

Throughout our work with images, Jesus moves in and through our cherished contexts and cultures, uniting us in our meditation and mission for a renewed global community of faith. The Christ we discover in and through the images challenges us to go out into the world and incarnate the selfsame Christ in our own situation, wherever that may be. It is a journey from meditation to proclamation and praxis. This is what mission is all about.

Appendix

Building a collection of images of Christ

A collection of images can easily be assembled by tapping into a variety of sources. Pictures of Christ can be cut out of Mission Society magazines and newspapers, or photocopied if permission has been given. The Church of England *Church Times* regularly prints religious pictures from recent publications, together with photographs of art in contemporary exhibitions and interesting new acquisitions in churches, including sculptures, stations of the cross, paintings, stained-glass windows, tapestries or other devotional imagery. The *Daily Telegraph* published an excellent six-part series, *AD. 2000 Years of Christianity*, to mark the Millennium (now in book form), while *Anglican World*, the quarterly journal of the Anglican Consultative Council, reproduces religious art and artefacts from different parts of the Anglican Communion. Another fruitful source is the recent spate of inexpensive publications featuring classical artists like Rembrandt, El Greco and Michelangelo. These contain quality reproductions of many of their religious works.

Books can be borrowed from libraries from both the art and the religious sections. Children's books often have colourful illustrations too. The internet is a new source of images with a number of sites to explore such as Google images. British church buildings have preserved a historic selection of sacred art and where permitted photographs can be taken. Art exhibitions in religious venues sometimes provide illustrated catalogues. Suitable postcards and posters can be found in museums, art galleries, specialist art shops, and cathedral and church book-shops. Christmas and Easter cards are another readily available source, as are calendars and prayer cards. The Benedictine nuns of Turvey Abbey in Essex have produced a useful collection of brightly coloured millennium cards, laminated sets of posters and illustrated booklets with meditations – *Jesus, Our Light*; *Jesus, Our Way*; *Jesus, Our Hope*; and *The Footsteps of Christ* – as well as a set of Stations.

In 1988 I started my own collection with a theology resource pack from Methodist Church Division of Ministries called *Discovering Jesus*, now out of print. This pack contained a selection of 22 postcards with suggestions for their use: games, ideas for worship, Bible studies and study units. More recently, the United Society for the Propagation of the Gospel, USPG Church of Ireland, Church Mission

Society and the Methodist Church have jointly produced a pack of images from around the world called *The Christ We Share* (1999, 2nd edition 2000). Described as 'A world church resource for local mission', it includes 32 A5 cards with 12 full-colour acetates for overhead projection, two booklets with theological information and explanatory notes on the images, activity sheets, ideas for worship and a resource list. This has been followed by a similar but smaller pack, *Born Among Us*, on the nativity. Both packs have been widely used in churches, schools and colleges.

Over the years, CAFOD (Catholic Agency for Overseas Development) has produced challenging material with a justice and humanitarian focus. Their distribution of the Miserior hangings, workbooks and meditations from Aachen in Germany are particularly effective in raising issues around the Suffering Christ and Christ the Liberator for group work. See, for example, the Lenten Veil *Hope for the Marginalised*, and the Haitian and Ethiopian hangings.

A congregation or faith community can build up its own resource pack by asking its members to collect pictures wherever they go and then pooling them. Holidays in Europe or any Catholic country provide the richest pickings with churches, museums, art galleries, and religious bookshops being the best places to look for images. Works of art from past centuries need to be balanced with both contemporary and international images. Taizé offers a selection of uncluttered images with an ecumenical dimension. Duplicates are always useful, especially with popular images such as Holman Hunt's *The Light of the World*, Albrecht Dürer's *Praying Hands*, and Margaret Tarrant's *The Loving Shepherd* together with her cards of Christ with children and animals, *Lesser Brethren*. Artistic merit is not an issue in the exercises.

In my collection I have 2,500 images which have been sorted into 250 packs according to the various gospel stories in which different people encountered Christ. Here we get to know Jesus as revealed through his relationships with children, Martha and Mary, the woman at the well, the woman taken in adultery, Mary Magdalene, the disciples being called and sent, Zacchaeus, Nicodemus, Peter, and so on. Other packs relate to Jesus' life and ministry: baptism, presentation in the Temple, temptation in the wilderness, wedding at Cana, calming a storm, walking on water, healing, teaching, feeding the multitudes, cleansing the Temple, Last Supper, every step of the passion story, resurrection appearances, ascension, and much more. Depending on the number of images available, both the number of packs concerning one story and the number of images in a pack vary considerably.

Now that I have returned to South Africa, I have created a permanent set of pictures of Christ featuring the multiracial mosaic of this rainbow nation, readily available for use in local church workshops. In the 'new' South Africa, these images are proving to be a vital tool in the ministry of crossing racial and cultural divides by creating respect for, and understanding of, our God-given differences. Even with a modest set of images it is possible to make up a set around a particular theme, and to use this for teaching, discussion and meditation. The focus may be cultural – Native American, Filipino, British, African or Indian. Or it may be historical – images relating to the Coptic, early Christian, Celtic or Renaissance periods. Or it may feature the work of one artist, a group of artists or artists from different countries. The most useful in a church context is to group images around biblical themes or the main liturgical events in the year.

Notes

1. Why Images of Christ?

1. John Bell, 'Our Image of Jesus' in *Present on Earth. Worship Resources on the Life of Jesus*, Iona Community: Wild Goose Publications 2002.

2. John Murray, 'Pictures of Christ', http://members.aol.com/RSISBELL/picture.html. 21 January 2001.

3. Doris Jean Dyke, *Crucified Woman*, Toronto: United Church Publishing House 1991, p. 47.

4. Leonide Ouspensky, *Theology of the Icon*, New York: St. Vladimir's Seminary Press, Crestwood 1978, pp. 9-10, 112.

5. Deborah Seddon, 'Elected silence, sing to me', *Church Times*, 26 November 1999. See also her *Gospel Icons*, Cambridge: Grove Books.

6. Deborah Seddon, 'Elected silence, sing to me', *Church Times*. 26 November 1999.

7. *Mission-shaped Church: church planting and fresh expressions of church in a changing context*, 2004 London: Church House Publishing 2004.

8. John Drane, *What is the New Age Still Saying to the Church?* London: Marshall Pickering 1999, pp. 181-2, 191-2.

9. John Drane, *What is the New Age Still Saying to the Church?* London: Marshall Pickering 1999, pp. 198-9.

10. Pete Ward, *Liquid Church*. Massachusetts: Hendrickson Publishers and Carlisle: Paternoster Press 2002.

11. Questions based on *Discovering Jesus*, Theological Pack 1, Methodist Church Division of Ministries.

2. Faith taking Flesh

1. Albert Dolan, Institute of Contextual Theology, n.d. p. 3.

2. Albert Dolan, Institute of Contextual Theology, n.d. pp. 1-3.

3. Albert Dolan, Institute of Contextual Theology, n.d. pp. 1-3.

4. John Pridmore, Diary', *Church Times.* 18 February 2000.

5. Nolan quoted by Larry Kaufmann, 'Good News to the Poor: the impact of Albert Nolan on Contextual Theology in South Africa', in McGlory Speckman and Larry Kaufman, (eds.), *Towards an Agenda for Contextual Theology. Essays in Honour of Albert Nolan,* Pietermaritzburg: Cluster Publications 2001, p. 7. See also Stephen Bevans, *Models of Contextual Theology.* Maryknoll: Orbis Books 1994, and Robert Schreiter, *Constructing Local Theologies,* London: SCM Press 1985.

6. Ernesto Cardenal, *Love in Practice. The Gospel in Solentiname,* London: Orbis Books and Search Press 1977.

7. Vincent Donavan, *Christianity Rediscovered. An epistle from the Masai,* London: SCM Press 1978.

8. Andrew Walls, 'The Translation Principle in Christian History', *The Missionary Movement in Christian History. Studies in the Transmission of Faith,* Maryknoll: Orbis Books and Edinburgh: T & T Clark 1996, pp. 22-27) and Andrew Walls, 'Vulnerable, interacting, incarnate faith' in *The Gospel and Our Culture,* Issue 26, Autumn 1999, p. 4.

9. Andrew Walls, 'The Translation Principle in Christian History', *The Missionary Movement in Christian History. Studies in the Transmission of* Faith, pp. 16-25, and Andrew Walls, 'Vulnerable, interacting, incarnate faith' in *The Gospel and Our Culture,* Issue 26, Autumn 1999, p. 4.

10. Gerald Arbuckle, *Earthing the Gospel. An Inculturation Handbook for Pastoral Workers,* London: Geoffrey Chapman 1990; Norbert Greinacher and Norbert Mette (eds.), *Christianity and cultures: a mutual enrichment,* Concilium 1994, No. 2, London: SCM Press 1994.

11. Anton Wessels, *Europe: Was it ever Really Christian? The interaction between gospel and culture,* London: SCM Press (translation from the Dutch) 1994, p. 3-15, 35-6, 47-54, 94-5, 154-8.

12. Anton Wessels, *Europe: Was it ever Really Christian? The interaction between gospel and culture,* pp. 3-15, 47-54, 94-95, 154-58.

13. Leonide Ouspensky, *Theology of the Icon*, New York: St. Vladimir's Seminary Press, Crestwood 1978, pp. 49, 68.

14. Leonide Ouspensky, *Theology of the Icon*, p. 70.

15. Anton Wessels, *Europe: Was it ever Really Christian? The interaction between gospel and culture*, p. 35-36; J.R. Porter, *Jesus Christ. The Jesus of History, the Christ of Faith*, London: Duncan Baird 1999, pp. 198-89.

16. Leonide Ouspensky, *Theology of the Icon*, pp. 83, 95.

17. Jaoslav Pelikan, *Jesus Through the Centuries. His Place in the History of Culture*, New York: Harper and Row 1987.

18. Jaoslav Pelikan, *Jesus Through the Centuries. His Place in the History of Culture*, pp. 2-3.

19. Jaoslav Pelikan, *Jesus Through the Centuries. His Place in the History of Culture*, pp. 220-31; cf. Heather Child and Dorothy Colles, *Christian Symbols Ancient and Modern*, London: G. Bell and Sons 1971, pp. 54-83.

20. Helen de Borchgrave, *A Journey into Christian Art*, Oxford: Lion 1999, pp. 188-92; Timothy Hyman, n.d. *Stanley Spencer. The Apotheosis of Love,* London: Barbican Art Gallery catalogue for an exhibition, p. 25; Timothy Hyman, and Patrick Wright, (eds.), *Stanley Spencer*, London: Tate Gallery Publishing for an exhibition, 2001, pp. 73, 202-5.

21. Timothy Hyman, n.d. *Stanley Spencer. The Apotheosis of Love.*

22. Timothy Hyman, n.d. *Stanley Spencer. The Apotheosis of Love.*

23. Timothy Hyman, n.d. *Stanley Spencer. The Apotheosis of Love.*

24. Dinah Roe Kendall, *Allegories of Heaven: an artist explores the 'Greatest Story Ever Told'*, London: Piquant 2002; cf. William Kurulek, *A Northern Nativity*, Montreal: Tundra Books 1976.

25. Peter Ball, *Icons of the Invisible* God, Newark: Chevron Books 1999.

26. *Stations: the new sacred art*, Bury St Edmund's Art Gallery 2000, pp. 12, 18.

27. Vincent Harding, 'Black Power and the American Christ' in Gayraud Wilmore and James Cone, *Black Theology: A Documentary History, 1966-1979*, Maryknoll: Orbis Books 1979, p. 37.

28. Laurie Goodstein, 'Image of a Black Jesus is spreading through African-American Churches', *International Herald Tribune,* 30 March 1994.

29. Lame Deer and Richard Erdoes, *Lame Deer: Sioux Medicine Man*, London: Davis Poynter 1973, p. 162.

30. Lame Deer and Richard Erdoes, *Lame Deer: Sioux Medicine Man*, p. 216.

31. Dina Cormick, Bernard Gcwensa and Ruben Xulu, Christian artists of Natal, Pretoria, Academia, p. 8.

32. Dr Kakhetla, Meseru.

33. *The Road to Damascus*, 1989, p. 8.

34. Jaroslav Pelikan, *Jesus Through the Centuries. His Place in the History of Culture.* New York: Harper and Row 1987.

3. Reaching People on the Edge

1. Laurie Green, *Let's Do Theology. A Pastoral Cycle Resource Book*, London: Mowbray 1990, p. 4.

2. David Bosch, *Transforming Mission. Paradigm Shifts in Theology of Mission.* Maryknoll: Orbis Books 1991, pp. 390-92, 519.

3. Robert Warren, *Building Missionary Congregations. Towards a post-modern way of being church*, London: Board of Mission Occasional Paper No. 4 1995, p.48.

4. Laurie Green, *Let's Do Theology. A Pastoral Cycle Resource Book.* London: Mowbray 1990; Philip Morris n.d. (c.1998). *Where do we go from here? Planning in your PCC*, A Church in Wales HELP! Booklet. Penarth: Church in Wales.

5. Christian Schwartz, *Natural Church Development. A Practical Guide to a New Approach*, Moggerhanger: British Church Growth Association 1998.

6. E.g. John Cole, *How to Be A Local Church*, Bury St Edmunds: Kevin Mayhew 1990; Philip Morris n.d. (c.1998). *Where do we go from here? Planning in your PCC*, A Church in Wales HELP! Booklet. Penarth: Church in Wales; Robert Warren and Janet Hodgson, *Growing Healthy Churches*, Oxford: Springboard 2001-2.

7. Laurie Green, *Let's Do Theology. A Pastoral Cycle Resource Book*, London: Mowbray 1990, pp. 74-98.

8. Laurie Green, *Let's Do Theology. A Pastoral Cycle Resource Book*, p.103.

9. Based on *Discovering Jesus*, Methodist Church Theological Resource Pack 1.

10. Based on *Discovering Jesus*, Methodist Church Theological Resource Pack 1.

11. Based on *Discovering Jesus*, Methodist Church Theological Resource Pack 1.

4. Moving Beyond Words

1. Philip Thomas, 'An Indian Summer of the Heart. An "Anthology of Affirmation" ', unpublished MS, Durham 1993, pp. 31, 34.

2. Stephen Barton, *The Spirituality of the Gospels*, London: SPCK 1992, p. 1.

3. Stephen Barton, *The Spirituality of the Gospels*, London: SPCK 1992, pp. 1-2.

4. Janet Hodgson, 'Proclaiming, Celebrating and Following Christ as the Paradigm of Change in People, Church and Society' in *By Word and Deed. Sharing the Good News through Mission,* edited by Colin Craston, London: Church Publishing House for the Anglican Communion 1992, pp. 15-16.

5. David Hay and Kate Hunt, 'Understanding the spirituality of people who don't go to church', A report on the findings of the Adults' Spirituality Project at the University of Nottingham 2000, www.martynmission.cam/BIAMSHay.htm

6. David Hay and Kate Hunt, 'Understanding the spirituality of people who don't go to church', A report on the findings of the Adults' Spirituality Project at the University of Nottingham 2000, pp. 12-14: www.martynmission.cam/BIAMSHay.htm

7. Jay Kothare, *Cry Amen not Halleluia. The Gospel according to the Black Inner-City Ghetto*, London: USPG Thinking Mission, Issue 22, 6 April 1995, p. 6.

8. Cf. Desmond Tutu, *God Has A Dream. A Vision of Hope for our Time*, London: Rider 2004.

9. Anthony de Mello, *Sadhana. A Way to God*, Anand, India: Gujarat Sahitya Prakash 1998, p. 66.

10. Simon Parke, *The Church Times.*

11. Anthony de Mello, *Sadhana. A Way to God*, Anand, India: Gujarat Sahitya Prakash 1998; Bede Griffiths, *The New Creation in Christ. Meditation and Community*, London: Darton, Longman and Todd 1992, pp. 64-65; John Main, *Word into Silence*, New York: Paulist Press 1981; John Main, *The Present Christ*, London: Darton, Longman and Todd 1985; Thomas Merton, *Contemplative Prayer* (New York: Herder and Herder 1969) Edition cited Image Books, Doubleday 1971.

12. Bede Griffiths, *The New Creation in Christ. Meditation and Community*, London: Darton, Longman and Todd 1992, pp. 64-65.

13. John Main, *Word into Silence*, New York: Paulist Press 1981; Neil McKenty, *In The Stillness Dancing. The Journey of John Main*, London: Dartman, Longman and Todd 1986, p. 159.

14.   Neil McKenty, *In The Stillness Dancing. The Journey of John Main*, London: Dartman, Longman and Todd 1986, p. 102.

15.   Billy Kennedy, Personal communication, 13 April 2005.

16.   Billy Kennedy, Personal communication, 13 April 2005.

17.   Billy Kennedy, Personal communication, 13 April 2005.

18.   Desmond Tutu, *God Has A Dream. A Vision of Hope for our Time*, London: Rider 2004, p. 109.

5. Enlarging our Vision of Christ

1.   Robert Cooper, Personal communication (Assistant Chaplain to Arts and Recreation, Durham Diocese), 20 July 2005.

2.   Roger Wollen, *The Methodist Church Collection of Modern Christian Art: An Introduction*, 2000 (reprinted 2004).

3.   Neil McGregor, 'How we see Jesus', *The Daily Telegraph*. 19 February 2000.

4.   Neil McGregor, 'How we see Jesus', *The Daily Telegraph*. 19 February 2000.

5.   Neil McGregor, 'How we see Jesus', *The Daily Telegraph*. 19 February 2000.

6.   *Images of Salvation,* Ashworth 2004, p. 16.

7.   Robert Cooper, Personal communication (Assistant Chaplain to Arts and Recreation, Durham Diocese), 20 July 2005.

8.   Richard Ellis, Diocesan Communications Officer for Lichfield, quoted in Andrew Carey, 'Tearing their hair out', *Church of England Newspaper*, 13 March 1998.

9.   Robert Cooper, Personal communication (Assistant Chaplain to Arts and Recreation, Durham Diocese), 20 July 2005.

10.   Stephen Bevans and Roger Schroeder, *Constants in Context. A Theology of Mission for Today*, Maryknoll: Orbis Books 2004.

11.   Andrew Atagotaaluk, 'Christianity and Traditional Culture' in *Bridges in Understanding. Aboriginal Christian Men Tell their* Stories, ed. Joyce Carlson and Alf Dumont, Toronto: Anglican Book Centre Publishing 2003, p. 115.

12.   Andrew Atagotaaluk, 'Christ the Carver' in *The Journey: Stories and Prayers for the Christian Year from People of the First Nations*, ed. Joyce Carlson, Toronto: Anglican Book Centre Publishing 1991, pp. 105-6.

13. Andrew Atagotaaluk, 'Christ the Carver' in *The Journey: Stories and Prayers for the Christian Year from People of the First Nations*, pp. 106-7.

14. T.S. Maluleke, 'What Africans are doing to Jesus: will he ever be the same again?' in Du Toit 1997, p. 200.

15. J.N.J. Kritzinger, 'A Question of Mission – A Mission of Questions' in *Missionalia*, vol. 30 no. 1, April 2002, p. 167.

16. Frans Claerhout, *It Could Happen Here*, Bloomfontein: Dreyer Publishers 1998; D. and D. Schwager, *Claerhout: Artist and Priest*, Maseru, Visual Publications 1994.

17. Masao Takenako, *Christian Art in Asia*, Japan: Kyo Bun Kwan with Christian Conference of Asia 1975, pp. 26-27.

18. Jacqueline Grant, ' "Come to my help Lord for I'm in trouble": Womanist Jesus and the Mutual Struggle for Liberation', *Journal of Black Theology in South Africa* Vol.8, No.1: May 1994, pp. 21-34.

19. Robert Cooper, Personal communication (Assistant Chaplain to Arts and Recreation, Durham Diocese), 20 July 2005.

20. Doris Jean Dyke, *Crucified Woman*, Toronto: United Church Publishing House 1991, p. 55.

21. Philip and Sally Scharper (ed.), *The Gospel in Art by The Peasants of Solentiname*, Maryknoll: Orbis Books 1984.

22. Teresa Hinga, 'Jesus Christ and the Liberation of Women in Africa' in Oduyoye and Kanyoro 1995, pp. 183-194.

23. Chung Hyun Kyung, *Struggle to be the Sun Again. Introducing Asian Women's Theology*, Maryknoll: Orbis Books 1990: pp. 53-57, 62-63.

24. Masao Takenaka and Ron O' Grady, *The Bible through Asian Eyes*, Auckland, Pace Publishing with Asian Christian Art Association 1991, p. 154.

25. Masao Takenaka and Ron O' Grady, *The Bible through Asian Eyes*, p. 155.

26. Chung Hyun Kyung, *Struggle to be the Sun Again. Introducing Asian Women's Theology*, p.62; see also Aruna Gnanadason, 'A spirituality that sustains us in our struggles', *International Review of Mission*, Vol.LXXX, No. 317, January 1991, pp. 29-34.

27. Chung Hyun Kyung, *Struggle to be the Sun Again. Introducing Asian Women's Theology*, pp. 138-39.

28. Ron O'Grady, *Christ for all people. Celebrating a World of Christian Art,* Geneva: WCC Publications 2001, pp. 102-3.

29. *From Darkness to Light, From Crown of Thorns to Victory,* in Ron O'Grady, *Christ for all people. Celebrating a World of Christian Art,* p. 151.

30. Ron O'Grady, *Christ for all people. Celebrating a World of Christian Art,* p. 132-33.

31. Ron O'Grady, *Christ for all people. Celebrating a World of Christian Art,* p. 30-31.

32. Ron O'Grady, *Christ for all people. Celebrating a World of Christian Art,* p. 107.

33. Doris Jean Dyke, *Crucified Woman,* Toronto: United Church Publishing House 1991, p. 41.

34. Doris Jean Dyke, *Crucified Woman,* p. 41.

35. Doris Jean Dyke, *Crucified Woman,* pp. 3-9, 15, 29-30, 63-74.

36. *Stations: the new sacred art,* Bury St Edmund's Art Gallery 2000, p. 18.

37. Bartolome Espartero, 'Minjung Messiah and the Filipino Christ: emerging images of Christ in Asia'. Unpublished dissertation, Diploma in Mission Studies, Selly Oak Colleges, Birmingham 1993.

38. *Seeing Salvation* 2000, p. 330-35; Helen de Borchgrave, *A Journey into Christian Art.* Oxford: Lion 1999.

Index to the Companion CD-ROM

How to use the CD-ROM

On a PC or Mac: place the CD into the computer's CD or DVD drive. The CD should start automatically. If not, select 'My Computer' and then double-click on the icon for your CD/DVD drive.

If you have never loaded PowerPoint Viewer before, this will auto-install and then you should see the title screen of *The Faith We See*. Click on 'Click to Enter' and then follow the instructions.

Clicking on any of the index images will take you to that particular image.

On a DVD player: the CD-ROM will also work on a domestic DVD player that supports the JPEG format. Place the CD in the drive as normal and press 'Play'. Then use the advance button to move to the next image. If this does not work, check the instructions supplied with your DVD player. You cannot use any of the indexing facilities in this mode.

Copyright information:

Please note that the images on this CD-ROM are copyright. Permission is given for one-off use for private viewing or projecting the images in public worship, although not for printing. Images may not be reproduced for commercial use or resale.

North-East images

9. Whalton Christ
[Photograph © Robert Cooper]
This image is made up of a collage of 2,850 individual pictures celebrating village life in Whalton, Northumberland. Here the face of Christ is seen in and through and among the people of God and God's creation. How do we respond?

12. Durham Miners' Gala
[Photograph © Robert Cooper]
The Durham miners' banners were a symbol of identity and belonging to a particular pit. Most featured political or socialist themes but a good number were religious. What does this say about faith and life?

11. Paul Judson, 'Living Stones'
[© Paul Judson]
Christ is incarnated in the ancient stones of Durham Cathedral, painted while Paul was an ordinand at Cranmer Hall, Durham. How do we see Christ incarnated where we are?

20. AIDS icon commissioned by the Chaplaincy to the Arts and Recreation. Design and calligraphy by Ewan Clayton. Woodwork by Peter Jones.
[© Bishop of Durham's AIDS Ministry Group. Photograph © Robert Cooper]
The figures read 'Christ has AIDS', raising a number of issues for discussion, reflection, prayer and action.

10. Fenwick Lawson, 'The Ascended Christ'
[Photograph © Robert Cooper]
The elemental and rough nature of this lifesize sculpture offers us a way of experiencing both the humanity and the transcendent spirituality of Christ.

South African Images

8. Contemporary South African Crucifixion
During the troubled times of the apartheid years, black people identified with the suffering Christ. What does the crucifixion mean to us?

16. 'Who bombed St Joseph's Catholic Church?' Phokeng nr Rustenburg, South Africa.
A graphic depiction of the desecration experienced during the liberation struggle in South Africa. Where is this still happening today, and how do we identify with it?

2. Jan Haen, 'Woman taken in adultery' by Jan Haen
Published in *Challenge* magazine no. 53, April/May 1999, South Africa. Used by permission of *Challenge*.
This image is particularly poignant in that the woman depicted was in fact stoned to death because she had AIDS, adding another dimension to the familiar story in which all of us can be seen as sinners.

5. Br Richard Maidwell, CSSR, 'Christ Meets Buddha', Temenos Retreat Centre, McGregor, South Africa.
[© Christine Lawley]
This wall painting would provide a good starting point for discussions about Christianity and other faiths.

1. Barbed Wire Crucifix, South Africa

The original crucifix was fashioned in a workshop with young black people during the liberation struggle in the 1980s, but it is an image that transcends all time and place. How does it speak to us?

Women's Images

3. Botswana Tree Trunk Crucifix

This image links crucifixion with incarnation and creation. At the same time, it allows us freedom to interpret it as we wish.

7. Nicol Matthee (aged 13), 'Jesus with Children'

[Nicol is now an arts student at Stellenbosch University. Permission given by Mrs Matthee]

Jesus with children is another popular image, here depicted by a young person. What are her insights and how do they resonate with ours?

19. Gillian Bell-Richards, 'The Temptation of Christ in the Wilderness'

[© Gillian Bell Richards]

The contemporary nature of this image means that we can personally identify with Christ in the wilderness. How does his desert experience resonate with ours?

18. Michelle Bootle, 'The Naked Christ'

[© Michelle Bootle]

In their re-imaging of Christ, women around the world bring fresh insights and challenges to our faith. How do we respond?

17. Sr Gereon Custodis, 'The Risen Lord', Mariannhill Mission, SA

[© Sr Gereon Custodis]

Much of the Christological imagery in Africa is found in tapestry. How do we experience a black Christ?

Different Themes

6. Christ the Good Shepherd

[source unknown]

The Good Shepherd is the earliest known image of Christ. Discuss why you think it is one of the most popular images in workshops today.

14. Meek. Mild. As If
[© Churches Advertising Network]
CAN has tried to communicate a more contemporary message and to make church seem more accessible to the wider public. Do you think they are succeeding?

13. St George's Tufnell Park, 'Christ in Community'
[© Simon Lord]
Affixed to the outer wall of the church, this icon gives visible expression to its vision of mission – that the Christian faith is found and lived in community.
What would our visual mission statement be?

15. Robert Lentz, ofm, 'The Christ of the Desert'
[© Robert Lentz 1990. Courtesy of Trinity Stores: www.trinitystores.com
001 800 699 4482]
This is particularly interesting with regard to thinking about Christ in an inter-faith/inter-cultural context.

4. Icon
The Transfiguration
[© Derek Bird]
Inspired by an early fifteenth-century Russian icon, the transfiguration experience of Jesus on the mountain top is expressed through a wealth of symbols: indigo (the kingdom of God), blue (the love of God), gold (Eternal Light), three shafts of light (the Holy Spirit, springs of living water). Can you identify the part played by all the figures/actors in this dramatic representation of the gospel story?